Introductory Message From the Office of Inspector General

The U.S. Department of Health and Human Services (HHS) Office of Inspector General (OIG) *Work Plan* for fiscal year (FY) 2015 summarizes new and ongoing reviews and activities that OIG plans to pursue with respect to HHS programs and operations during the current fiscal year and beyond.

What is our responsibility?

Our organization was created to protect the integrity of HHS programs and operations and the well-being of beneficiaries by detecting and preventing fraud, waste, and abuse; identifying opportunities to improve program economy, efficiency, and effectiveness; and holding accountable those who do not meet program requirements or who violate Federal health care laws. Our mission encompasses more than 100 programs administered by HHS at agencies such as the Centers for Medicare & Medicaid Services, Administration for Children and Families, Centers for Disease Control and Prevention, Food and Drug Administration, and National Institutes of Health.

The amount of work conducted in each category is set by the purpose limitations in the money appropriated to OIG. OIG's funding that is directed toward oversight of the Medicare and Medicaid programs constitutes a significant portion of its total funding (approximately 76 percent in 2014). The remaining share of OIG's efforts and resources focuses on HHS's other programs and management processes, including key issues such as the accuracy of financial assistance payments and the efficient and effective operation of health insurance marketplaces, safety of the nation's food and drug supply, security of national stockpiles of pharmaceuticals for use during emergencies, and the integrity of contracts and grants management processes and transactions.

How and where do we operate?

Our staff members are deployed throughout the Nation in regional and field offices and in the Washington, DC, headquarters. We conduct audits, evaluations, and investigations; provide guidance to industry; and, when appropriate, impose civil monetary penalties (CMPs), assessments, and administrative sanctions. We collaborate with HHS and its operating and staff divisions, the Department of Justice (DOJ) and other executive branch agencies, Congress, and States to bring about systemic changes, successful prosecutions, negotiated settlements, and recovery of funds. The following are descriptions of our mission-based components.

- **The Office of Audit Services (OAS)**. OAS provides auditing services for HHS, either by conducting audits with its own resources or by overseeing audit work done by others. Audits examine the performance of HHS programs and/or its grantees and contractors in carrying out their respective responsibilities and are intended to provide independent assessments of HHS programs and operations. These assessments help reduce waste, abuse, and mismanagement and promote economy and efficiency throughout HHS.

- **The Office of Evaluation and Inspections (OEI).** OEI conducts national evaluations to provide HHS, Congress, and the public with timely, useful, and reliable information on significant issues. These evaluations focus on preventing fraud, waste, and abuse and promoting economy, efficiency, and effectiveness in HHS programs. OEI reports also present practical recommendations for improving program operations.

- **The Office of Investigations (OI)**. OI conducts criminal, civil, and administrative investigations of fraud and misconduct related to HHS programs, operations, and beneficiaries. With investigators working in almost every State and the District of Columbia, OI coordinates with DOJ and other Federal, State, and local law enforcement authorities. OI also coordinates with OAS and OEI when audits and evaluations uncover potential fraud. OI's investigative efforts often lead to criminal convictions, administrative sanctions, or CMPs.

- **The Office of Counsel to the Inspector General (OCIG)**. OCIG provides general legal services to OIG, rendering advice and opinions on HHS programs and operations and providing all legal support for OIG's internal operations. OCIG represents OIG in all civil and administrative fraud and abuse cases involving HHS programs, including False Claims Act, program exclusion, and CMP cases. In connection with these cases, OCIG also negotiates and monitors corporate integrity agreements. OCIG renders advisory opinions, issues compliance program guidance, publishes fraud alerts, and provides other guidance to the health care industry concerning the anti-kickback statute and other OIG enforcement authorities.

The organizational entities described above are supported by the Immediate Office of the Inspector General and the Office of Management and Policy.

How do we plan our work?

Work planning is a dynamic process, and adjustments are made throughout the year to meet priorities and to anticipate and respond to emerging issues with the resources available. We assess relative risks in the programs for which we have oversight authority to identify the areas most in need of attention and, accordingly, to set priorities for the sequence and proportion of resources to be allocated. In evaluating proposals for the *Work Plan*, we consider a number of factors, including:

- mandatory requirements for OIG reviews, as set forth in laws, regulations, or other directives;
- requests made or concerns raised by Congress, HHS management, or the Office of Management and Budget;
- top management and performance challenges facing HHS;
- work performed by partner organizations;
- management's actions to implement our recommendations from previous reviews; and
- timeliness.

What do we accomplish?

For FY 2014, we reported expected recoveries of over $4.9 billion, consisting of nearly $834.7 million in audit receivables and about $4.1 billion in investigative receivables, which include about $1.1 billion in non-HHS investigative receivables resulting from our work in areas such as the States' shares of Medicaid restitution. We also identified about $15.7 billion in savings estimated for FY 2014 on the basis of prior-period legislative, regulatory, or administrative actions that were supported by OIG recommendations. Such estimates generally reflect third-party projections (such as those by the Congressional Budget Office or HHS actuaries) made at the time the action was taken. Actual savings may be higher or lower.

We reported FY 2014 exclusions of 4,017 individuals and entities from participation in Federal health care programs; 971 criminal actions against individuals or entities that engaged in crimes against HHS programs; and 533 civil actions, which include false claims and unjust-enrichment lawsuits filed in Federal district court, CMP settlements, and administrative recoveries related to provider self-disclosure matters.

A Note About This Edition:

This edition of the *Work Plan*, effective as of October 2014, describes OIG audits, evaluations, and certain legal and investigative initiatives that are ongoing. The word "new" after a project title indicates that the project did not appear in the previous *Work Plan*. For each project, we include the subject, primary objective, and criteria related to the topic. At the end of each description, we provide the internal identification code for the review (if a number has been assigned) and the year in which we expect one or more reports to be issued as a result of the review.

This edition also forecasts areas for which OIG anticipates planning and/or beginning work in the upcoming fiscal year and beyond. Typically, these broader areas of focus are based on the results of OIG's risk assessments and have been identified as significant management and performance challenges facing HHS. In FY 2015 and beyond, we will continue to focus on emerging payment, eligibility, management, and IT systems security vulnerabilities in health care reform programs, such as the health insurance marketplaces. OIG plans to add to its portfolio of work on care quality and access in Medicare and Medicaid, as well as on public health and human services programs. OIG's examination of the appropriateness of Medicare and Medicaid payments will continue, with possible additional work on the efficiency and effectiveness of payment policies and practices in inpatient and outpatient settings, for prescription drugs, and in managed care. Other areas under consideration for new work include, for example, the integrity of the food, drug, and medical device supply chains; the security of electronic data; the use and exchange of health information technology; and emergency preparedness and response efforts.

OIG will periodically update its online *Work Plan*, available at www.oig.hhs.gov.

The body of the *Work Plan* is followed by Appendix A, which describes our reviews related to the Patient Protection and Affordable Care Act of 2010 and Appendix B, which describes our oversight of the funding that HHS received under the American Recovery and Reinvestment Act of 2009.

Because we make continuous adjustments to the *Work Plan* as appropriate, we do not provide status reports on the progress of the reviews. However, if you have other questions about this publication, please contact us at public.affairs@oig.hhs.gov.

OIG on the Web: http://www.oig.hhs.gov

Follow us on Twitter: http://twitter.com/OIGatHHS

Contents

Medicaid Program 28

CMS-Related Legal and Investigative Activities 43

Public Health Reviews 47

Other HHS-Related Reviews 59

Appendixes

Medicare Part A covers certain inpatient services in hospitals and skilled nursing facilities (SNF) and some home health services. Medicare Part B covers designated practitioners' services; outpatient care; and certain other medical services, equipment, supplies, and drugs that Part A does not cover. The Centers for Medicare & Medicaid Services (CMS) uses Medicare Administrative Contractors (MACs) to administer Medicare Part A and Medicare Part B and to process claims for both parts.

The Office of Inspector General (OIG) has identified reducing waste in Medicare Parts A and B and ensuring quality, including in nursing home, hospice care, and home- and community-based care, as top management challenges facing the Department. OIG has focused its efforts on reducing improper payments, improving quality and access, and fostering economical payment policies. Work planning for fiscal year (FY) 2015 and beyond will consider the following:

Quality of Care: Planned work will examine settings in which OIG has identified gaps in program safeguards intended to ensure medical necessity, patient safety, and quality of care. We will also continue our focus on access to care, including beneficiary access to durable medical equipment, prosthetics, orthotics, and supplies in the context of new programs involving competitive bidding.

Appropriate Payments: Planning is ongoing to expand OIG's portfolio examining inefficient payment policies or practices, including comparison among Government programs to identify instances when Medicare paid significantly different amounts for the same or similar services or when less efficient payment methodologies were used. Planning is ongoing for work addressing Medicare costs incurred because of deficiencies in services or defective medical devices, as well as noncompliance or other vulnerabilities in care settings with high payment error rates.

Oversight of Payment and Delivery Reform: Planning is underway to expand OIG's work addressing changes to Medicare programs designed to improve efficiency and quality of care and to promote program integrity and transparency. OIG will consider work examining the transition from volume- to value-based payments and the soundness and effectiveness of the payment structures, care coordination, and administration of these new payment models. Work expected to begin in 2015 and beyond includes examinations of data and metrics to document and measure quality and performance.

Hospitals

Acronyms and Abbreviations for Selected Terms:

CMS—Centers for Medicare & Medicaid Services
CoP—conditions of participation (in Medicare)
DRG—diagnosis related group
FTE—full-time-equivalent

GME—graduate medical education
IME—indirect medical education
PPS—prospective payment system
SNF—skilled nursing facility

Hospital-Related Policies and Practices

➤ Reconciliations of outlier payments

We will review Medicare outlier payments to hospitals to determine whether CMS performed necessary reconciliations in a timely manner to enable Medicare contractors to perform final settlement of the hospitals' associated cost reports. We will also determine whether the Medicare contractors referred all hospitals that meet the criteria for outlier reconciliations to CMS. Outliers are additional payments that Medicare provides to hospitals for beneficiaries who incur unusually high costs. CMS reconciles outlier payments on the basis of the most recent cost-to-charge ratio from hospitals' associated cost reports. Outlier payments also may be adjusted to reflect the time value of money for overpayments and underpayments. Without timely reconciliations and final settlements, the cost reports remain open and funds may not be properly returned to the Medicare Trust Fund. (42 CFR, § 412.84(i)(4).) (OAS; W-00-13-35451; W-00-14-35451; various reviews; expected issue date: FY 2015)

➤ New inpatient admission criteria

We will determine the impact of new inpatient admission criteria on hospital billing, Medicare payments, and beneficiary copayments. This review will also determine how billing varied among hospitals in FY 2014. Previous OIG work identified millions of dollars in overpayments to hospitals for short inpatient stays that should have been billed as outpatient stays. Beginning in FY 2014, new criteria state that physicians should admit for inpatient care those beneficiaries who are expected to need at least 2 nights of hospital care (known as the "two midnight policy"). Beneficiaries whose care is expected to last fewer than 2 nights should be treated as outpatients. The criteria represent a substantial change in the way hospitals bill for inpatient and outpatient stays. (OEI; 00-00-00000; expected issue date: FY 2016)

➤ Medicare costs associated with defective medical devices

We will review Medicare claims to identify the costs resulting from additional use of medical services associated with defective medical devices and determine the impact of the cost on the Medicare Trust Fund. CMS has previously expressed concerns about the impact of the cost of replacement devices, including ancillary cost, on Medicare payments for inpatient and outpatient services. (OAS; W-00-13-35516; various reviews; expected issue date: FY 2015)

➤ Analysis of salaries included in hospital cost reports

We will review data from Medicare cost reports and hospitals to identify salary amounts included in operating costs reported to and reimbursed by Medicare. We will determine the potential impact on the Medicare Trust Fund if the amount of employee compensation that could be submitted to Medicare for reimbursement on future cost reports had limits. Employee compensation may be included in allowable provider costs only to the extent that it represents reasonable remuneration for managerial, administrative, professional, and other services related to the operation of the facility and furnished in connection with patient care. (CMS's *Provider Reimbursement Manual*, Part 1, Pub. No. 15-1, Ch. 9 § 902.2.) Medicare does not provide any specific limits on the salary amounts that can be reported on the hospital cost report. (OAS; W-00-14-35713; expected issue date: FY 2015)

Medicare oversight of provider-based status

We will determine the extent to which provider-based facilities meet CMS's criteria. Provider-based status allows facilities owned and operated by hospitals to bill as hospital outpatient departments. Provider-based status can result in higher Medicare payments for services furnished at provider-based facilities and may increase beneficiaries' coinsurance liabilities. In 2011, the Medicare Payment Advisory Commission (MedPAC) expressed concerns about the financial incentives presented by provider-based status and stated that Medicare should seek to pay similar amounts for similar services. (OEI; 04-12-00380; expected issue date: FY 2015)

Comparison of provider-based and free-standing clinics

We will review and compare Medicare payments for physician office visits in provider-based clinics and free-standing clinics to determine the difference in payments made to the clinics for similar procedures and assess the potential impact on the Medicare program of hospitals' claiming provider-based status for such facilities. Provider-based facilities often receive higher payments for some services than do freestanding clinics. The requirements to be met for a facility to be treated as provider based are at 42 CFR § 413.65(d). (OAS; W-00-14-35724; W-00-15-35724; expected issue date: FY 2015)

Critical access hospitals—Payment policy for swing-bed services

We will compare reimbursement for swing-bed services at critical access hospitals (CAHs) to the same level of care obtained at traditional SNFs to determine whether Medicare could achieve cost savings through a more cost effective payment methodology. Swing beds are inpatient beds that can be used interchangeably for either acute care or skilled nursing services. The Balanced Budget Act of 1997 (BBA) created the CAH Program to ensure access to health care services in rural areas. The Medicare Prescription Drug, Improvement, and Modernization Act of 2003 (MMA) allowed CAHs to receive Medicare reimbursement equal to 101 percent of reasonable cost and have up to 25 inpatient beds that could be used for acute care or swing-bed services, with CMS approval. (Social Security Act, § 1814(l).) Neither the BBA nor the MMA established any length-of-stay limits for the use of swing-beds. Unlike CAHs, traditional SNFs are reimbursed under a prospective payment system (PPS) through case-mix, adjusted per-diem prospective payment rates for all SNFs. The payment rates represent payment in full for all costs associated with furnishing covered SNF services to Medicare beneficiaries. (OAS; W-00-12-35101; W-00-13-35101; W-00-14-35101; various reviews; expected issue date: FY 2015)

Hospitals—Billing and Payments

Inpatient claims for mechanical ventilation

We will review Medicare payments for inpatient hospital claims with certain Medicare Severity-Diagnosis Related Group (MS-DRG) assignments that require mechanical ventilation to determine whether hospitals' DRG assignments and resultant Medicare payments were appropriate. Mechanical ventilation is the use of a ventilator or respirator to take over active breathing for a patient. Claims must be completed accurately to be processed correctly and promptly. (CMS's *Medicare Claims Processing Manual*, Pub. No. 100 04, ch. 1, § 80.3.2.2.) For certain DRGs to qualify for Medicare coverage, a patient must receive 96 or more hours of mechanical ventilation. Our review will include claims for beneficiaries who received over 96 hours of mechanical ventilation. Previous OIG reviews identified improper payments made because hospitals inappropriately billed for beneficiaries who did not receive 96 or more hours of mechanical ventilation. (OAS; W-00-14-35575; various reviews; expected issue date: FY 2015)

➢ Selected inpatient and outpatient billing requirements

We will review Medicare payments to acute care hospitals to determine hospitals' compliance with selected billing requirements and recommend recovery of overpayments. Prior OIG audits, investigations, and inspections have identified areas at risk for noncompliance with Medicare billing requirements. Our review will focus on those hospitals with claims that may be at risk for overpayments. (OAS; W-00-12-35538; W-00-13-35538; W-00-14-35538; W-00-15-35538; various reviews; expected issue date: FY 2015)

➢ Duplicate graduate medical education payments

We will review provider data from CMS's Intern and Resident Information System to determine whether hospitals received duplicate or excessive graduate medical education (GME) payments. We will also assess the effectiveness of IRIS in preventing duplicate payments for GME costs. If duplicate payments were claimed, we will determine which payment was appropriate. Prior OIG reviews have determined that hospitals have received duplicate reimbursement for GME costs. Medicare pays teaching hospitals for direct graduate medical education (DGME) and indirect medical education (IME) costs. When payments for DGME and IME costs are being calculated, no intern or resident may be counted by Medicare as more than one full-time-equivalent (FTE) employee. (42 CFR §§ 413.78(b) and 412.105(f)(1)(iii).) The primary purpose of IRIS is to ensure that no intern or resident is counted as more than one FTE. (OAS; W-00-13-35432; various reviews; expected issue date: FY 2015)

➢ Indirect medical education payments

We will review provider data to determine whether hospitals' IME payments were made in accordance with Federal regulations and guidelines. We will determine whether the IME payments were calculated properly. Prior OIG reviews have determined that hospitals have received excess reimbursement for IME costs. Teaching hospitals with residents in approved GME programs receive additional payments for each Medicare discharge to reflect the higher indirect patient care costs of teaching hospitals relative to those of nonteaching hospitals. (42 U.S.C. § 1395ww(d)(5)(B).) The additional payments, known as the IME adjustments, are calculated using the hospital's ratio of resident FTEs to available beds. (OAS; W-00-14-35722; W-00-15-35722; expected issue date: FY 2015)

➢ Outpatient dental claims

We will review Medicare hospital outpatient payments for dental services to determine whether such payments were made in accordance with Medicare requirements. Current OIG audits have indicated that hospitals received Medicare reimbursement for noncovered dental services, resulting in significant overpayments. Dental services are generally excluded from Medicare coverage, with a few exceptions. (Social Security Act, § 1862(a)(12).) For example, Medicare reimbursement is allowed for the extraction of teeth to prepare the jaw for radiation treatment (CMS's *Medicare Benefit Policy Manual*, Pub. No. 100-02, ch. 15, § 150). (OAS; W-00-14-35603; various reviews; expected issue date: FY 2015)

➤ Outpatient evaluation and management services billed at the new-patient rate

We will review Medicare outpatient payments made to hospitals for evaluation and management (E/M) services for clinic visits billed at the new-patient rate to determine whether they were appropriate and will recommend recovery of overpayments. Preliminary work identified overpayments that occurred because hospitals used new-patient codes when billing for services to established patients. The rate at which Medicare pays for E/M services requires hospitals to identify patients as either new or established, depending on previous encounters with the hospital. According to Federal regulations, the meaning of "new" and "established' pertains to whether the patient has been seen as a registered inpatient or outpatient of the hospital within the past 3 years. (73 Fed. Reg. 68679 (November 18, 2008).) (OAS; W-00-14-35627; expected issue date: FY 2015)

➤ Nationwide review of cardiac catheterizations and endomyocardial biopsies

We will review Medicare payments for right heart catheterizations (RHC) and endomyocardial biopsies billed during the same operative session and determine whether hospitals complied with Medicare billing requirements. Previous OIG reviews have identified inappropriate payments when hospitals were paid for separate RHC procedures when the services were already included in payments for endomyocardial biopsies. To be processed correctly and promptly, a bill must be completed accurately. (CMS's *Medicare Claims Processing Manual*, Pub. No. 100-04, ch. 1, §80.3.2.2.) (OAS; W-00-14-35721; various reviews; expected issue date: FY 2015)

➤ Payments for patients diagnosed with kwashiorkor

We will review Medicare payments made to hospitals for claims that include a diagnosis of kwashiorkor to determine whether the diagnosis is adequately supported by documentation in the medical record. To be processed correctly and promptly, a bill must be completed accurately. (CMS's *Medicare Claims Processing Manual*, Pub. No. 100-04, ch. 1, §80.3.2.2.) A diagnosis of kwashiorkor on a claim substantially increases the hospitals' reimbursement from Medicare. Kwashiorkor is a form of severe protein malnutrition that generally affects children living in tropical and subtropical parts of the world during periods of famine or insufficient food supply. It is typically not found in the United States. Prior OIG reviews have identified inappropriate payments to hospitals for claims with a kwashiorkor diagnosis. (OAS; W-00-13-35715; W-00-14-35715; various reviews; expected issue date: FY 2015)

➤ Bone marrow or stem cell transplants

We will review Medicare payments to hospitals for bone marrow or stem cell transplants to determine whether the payments were made in accordance with Federal rules and regulations. Bone marrow or peripheral blood stem cell transplantation includes mobilization, harvesting, and transplant of bone marrow or peripheral blood stem cells and the administration of high-dose chemotherapy or radiotherapy before the actual transplant. When bone marrow or peripheral blood stem cell transplantation is covered, all necessary steps are included in coverage. (CMS's *Medicare Claims Processing Manual*, Pub. No. 100-04, ch. 3, §90.3.) Bone marrow or stem cell transplants are covered under Medicare only for specific diagnoses. Procedure codes must be accompanied by the diagnosis codes that meet specified coverage criteria. Prior OIG reviews have identified hospitals that have incorrectly billed for bone marrow or stem cell transplants. (OAS; W-00-14-35723; expected issue date: FY 2015)

> Review of hospital wage data used to calculate Medicare payments (new)

We will review hospital controls over the reporting of wage data used to calculate wage indexes for Medicare payments. Prior OIG wage index work identified hundreds of millions of dollars in incorrectly reported wage data and resulted in policy changes by CMS with regard to how hospitals reported deferred compensation cost. Hospitals must accurately report wage data to CMS annually to develop wage index rates. (Social Security Act, §1886(d)(3) and 1886(d)(3)(E).) (OAS; W-00-14-35725; W-00-15-35725; various reviews; expected issue date: FY 2015)

Hospitals—Quality of Care and Safety

> Participation in projects with quality improvement organizations

We will determine the extent and nature of hospitals' participation in quality improvement projects with Quality Improvement Organizations (QIOs). We will also determine the extent to which QIOs' quality improvement projects in hospitals overlap with projects offered by other entities. CMS is required to enter into contracts with QIOs, formerly called utilization and quality control peer review organizations. (Social Security Act § 1862 (g).) The purpose of the QIOs is to improve the efficiency, effectiveness, economy, and quality of services delivered to Medicare beneficiaries. Medicare spent about $1.6 billion for QIOs' recently completed 3-year contract period, and each contract specifies clinical areas for quality improvement projects. (OEI; 01-12-00650; expected issue date: FY 2015)

> Oversight of pharmaceutical compounding

We will determine the extent to which Medicare's oversight of Medicare-participating acute care hospitals addresses recommended practices for pharmaceutical compounding oversight. Pharmaceutical compounding is the creation of a prescription drug tailored to meet the needs of an individual patient. Most hospitals compound at least some pharmaceuticals onsite. Medicare oversees the safety of pharmaceuticals compounded at Medicare-participating hospitals through the accreditation and certification process. This work is particularly important in view of a 2012 meningitis outbreak resulting from contaminated injections of compounded drugs. (OEI; 01-13-00400; expected issue date: FY 2015)

> Oversight of hospital privileging

We will determine how hospitals assess medical staff candidates before granting initial privileges, including verification of credentials and review of the National Practitioner Databank. Hospitals that participate in Medicare must have an organized medical staff that operates under bylaws approved by a governing body. (42 CFR § 482.22). A hospital's governing body must ensure that the members of the medical staff, including physicians and other licensed independent practitioners, are accountable for the quality of care provided to patients. Robust hospital privileging programs contribute to patient safety. (OEI; 06-13-00410; expected issue date: FY 2016)

> Inpatient rehabilitation facilities—Adverse events in post-acute care for Medicare beneficiaries

We will estimate the national incidence of adverse and temporary harm events for Medicare beneficiaries receiving postacute care in inpatient rehabilitation facilities (IRF). We will also identify factors contributing to these events, determine the extent to which the events were preventable, and estimate the associated costs to Medicare. IRFs are inpatient facilities that provide intensive rehabilitation therapy to patients recovering from illness, injury, or surgery, typically consisting of at least 3 hours of therapy per day. Upon discharge from the hospital, IRF residents often require extensive services to improve functioning before returning home. IRFs provide 11 percent of postacute facility care and have experienced rapid growth over the last decade. IRF care accounted for $7 billion in Medicare expenditures in 2011. (OEI; 06-14-00110; expected issue date: FY 2015)

➤ Long-term-care hospitals—Adverse events in post-acute care for Medicare beneficiaries (new)

We will estimate the national incidence of adverse and temporary harm events for Medicare beneficiaries receiving care in long-term-care hospitals (LTCHs). We will also identify factors contributing to these events, determine the extent to which the events were preventable, and estimate the associated costs to Medicare. LTCHs are inpatient hospitals that provide long-term care to clinically complex patients, such as those with multiple acute or chronic conditions. Medicare beneficiaries typically enter LTCHs following an acute-care hospital stay to receive intensive rehabilitation and medical care. LTCHs are the third most common type of post-acute care facility after SNFs and independent rehabilitation facilities (IRFs), accounting for nearly 11 percent of Medicare costs for post-acute care ($5.4 billion in FY 2011). (OEI; 06-14-00530; expected issue date: FY 2015)

Nursing Homes

Acronyms and Abbreviations for Selected Terms:

CMS—Centers for Medicare & Medicaid Services   SNF—skilled nursing facility

➤ Medicare Part A billing by skilled nursing facilities

We will describe changes in SNF billing practices from FYs 2011 to 2013. Prior OIG work found that SNFs increasingly billed for the highest level of therapy even though beneficiary characteristics remained largely unchanged. OIG also found that SNFs billed one-quarter of all 2009 claims in error; this erroneous billing resulted in $1.5 billion in inappropriate Medicare payments. CMS has made substantial changes to how SNFs bill for services for Medicare Part A stays. (OEI; 02-13-00610; various reviews; expected issue date: FY 2015)

➤ Questionable billing patterns for Part B services during nursing home stays

We will identify questionable billing patterns associated with nursing homes and Medicare providers for Part B services provided to nursing home residents during stays not paid under Part A (for example, stays during which benefits are exhausted or the 3-day prior-inpatient-stay requirement is not met). A series of studies will examine several broad categories of services, such as foot care. Congress directed OIG to monitor Part B billing for abuse during non-Part A stays to ensure that no excessive services are provided. (Medicare, Medicaid, and SCHIP Benefits Improvement and Protection Act of 2000, § 313.) (OEI; 06-14-00160; various reviews; expected issue date: FY 2015)

> ## State agency verification of deficiency corrections

We will determine whether State survey agencies verified correction plans for deficiencies identified during nursing home recertification surveys. A prior OIG review found that one State survey agency did not always verify that nursing homes corrected deficiencies identified during surveys in accordance with Federal requirements. Federal regulations require nursing homes to submit correction plans to the State survey agency or CMS for deficiencies identified during surveys. (42 CFR § 488.402(d).) CMS requires State survey agencies to verify the correction of identified deficiencies through onsite reviews or by obtaining other evidence of correction. (*State Operations Manual*, Pub. No. 100-07, § 7300.3.) (OAS; W-00-13-35701; W-00-14-35701; various reviews; expected issue date: FY 2015)

> ## Program for national background checks for long-term-care employees

We will review the procedures implemented by participating States for long-term-care facilities or providers to conduct background checks on prospective employees and providers who would have direct access to patients and determine the costs of conducting background checks. We will determine the outcomes of the States' programs and determine whether the programs led to any unintended consequences. Section 6201 of the Patient Protection and Affordable Care Act (ACA) requires the Secretary of Health and Human Services to carry out a nationwide program for States to conduct national and State background checks for prospective direct patient access employees of nursing facilities and other long-term-care providers. The program is administered by CMS. To carry out the nationwide program, CMS has issued solicitations for grant awards. All States, the District of Columbia, and U.S. territories are eligible to be considered for a grant award. OIG is required under the ACA to submit a report to Congress evaluating this program. This mandated work is ongoing and will be issued at the program's conclusion, as required. (ACA, § 6401.) (OEI; 07-10-00420; expected issue date: FY 2015; ACA)

> ## Hospitalizations of nursing home residents for manageable and preventable conditions

We will determine the extent to which Medicare beneficiaries residing in nursing homes are hospitalized as a result of conditions thought to be manageable or preventable in the nursing home setting. A 2013 OIG review found that 25 percent of Medicare beneficiaries were hospitalized for any reason in FY 2011. Hospitalizations of nursing home residents are costly to Medicare and may indicate quality-of-care problems in nursing homes. (OEI; 06-11-00041; expected issue date: FY 2015)

Hospices

Acronyms and Abbreviations for Selected Terms:

ALF—assisted living facility
CMS—Centers for Medicare & Medicaid Services

MedPAC—Medicare Payment Advisory Commission

Hospices in assisted living facilities

We will review the extent to which hospices serve Medicare beneficiaries who reside in assisted living facilities (ALFs). We will determine the length of stay, levels of care received, and common terminal illnesses of beneficiaries who receive hospice care in ALFs. Pursuant to the ACA, § 3132, CMS must reform the hospice payment system, collect data relevant to revising hospice payments, and develop quality measures for hospices. Our work is intended to provide HHS with information relevant to these requirements. Medicare covers hospice services for eligible beneficiaries under Medicare Part A. (Social Security Act, § 1812(a).) Hospice care may be provided to individuals and their families in various settings, including the beneficiary's place of residence, such as an ALF. ALF residents have the longest lengths of stay in hospice care. MedPAC has said that these long stays bear further monitoring and examination. (OEI; 02-14-00070; expected issue date: FY 2015; ACA)

Hospice general inpatient care

We will review the use of hospice general inpatient care. We will assess the appropriateness of hospices' general inpatient care claims and the content of election statements for hospice beneficiaries who receive general inpatient care. We will also review hospice medical records to address concerns that this level of hospice care is being misused. Hospice care is palliative rather than curative. When a beneficiary elects hospice care, the hospice agency assumes the responsibility for medical care related to the beneficiary's terminal illness and related conditions. Federal regulations address Medicare conditions of participation (CoP) for hospices. (42 CFR Part 418.) Beneficiaries may revoke their election of hospice care and return to standard Medicare coverage at any time. (42 CFR § 418.28.) (OEI; 02-10-00491; 02-10-00492; expected issue date: FY 2015)

Home Health Services

Acronyms and Abbreviations for Selected Terms:

CMS—Centers for Medicare & Medicaid Services   PPS—prospective payment system
HHA—home health agency

Home health prospective payment system requirements

We will review compliance with various aspects of the home health PPS, including the documentation required in support of the claims paid by Medicare. We will determine whether home health claims were paid in accordance with Federal laws and regulations. A prior OIG report found that one in four home health agencies (HHAs) had questionable billing. Further, CMS designated newly enrolling HHAs as high-risk providers, citing their record of fraud, waste, and abuse. Since 2010, nearly $1 billion in improper Medicare payments and fraud has been identified relating to the home health benefit. Home health services include part-time or intermittent skilled nursing care, as well as other skilled care services, such as physical, occupational, and speech therapy; medical social work; and home health aide services. (OAS; W-00-13-35501; W-00-14-35501; various reviews; expected issue date: FY 2015)

> ## Employment of individuals with criminal convictions

We will determine the extent to which HHAs employed individuals with criminal convictions. We will also examine the criminal convictions of selected employees with potentially disqualifying convictions. Federal law requires that HHAs comply with all applicable State and local laws and regulations. (Social Security Act, §1891(a)(5), implemented at 42 CFR § 484.12(a).) Nearly all States have laws prohibiting certain health-care-related entities from employing individuals with certain types of criminal convictions. (OEI; 07-14-00130; expected issue date: FY 2015)

Medical Equipment and Supplies

Acronyms and Abbreviations for Selected Terms:

CMS—Centers for Medicare & Medicaid Services
E/M—evaluation and management (services)

LCD—local coverage determination
PMD—power mobility device

Equipment and Supplies—Policies and Practices

> ### Power mobility devices—Lump-sum purchase versus rental

We will determine whether potential savings can be achieved by Medicare if certain power mobility devices (PMDs) are rented over a 13-month period rather than acquired through a lump-sum purchase. (OAS; W-00-14-35461; expected issue date: FY 2015)

> ### Competitive bidding for medical equipment items and services—Mandatory postaward audit

We will review the process CMS used to conduct competitive bidding and to make subsequent pricing determinations for certain medical equipment items and services in selected competitive bidding areas under rounds 1 and 2 of the competitive bidding program. Federal law requires OIG to conduct postaward audits to assess this process. (Medicare Improvements for Patients and Providers Act of 2008 (MIPPA), § 154(a)(1)(E).) (OAS; W-00-13-35241; various reviews; expected issued date: FY 2015)

> ### Competitive bidding for diabetes testing supplies—Market share review

We will determine the market share of different types of diabetes test strips for the 3-month period of October through December 2013. MIPPA requires that, in rounds subsequent to the round 1 rebid of the competitive bidding program, contracts for mail order diabetes test strips be awarded to suppliers that provide at least 50 percent, by volume, of all types of diabetic testing strips. CMS requested this study and may use the results for program analysis purposes and for evaluating the effect of the competitive bidding program on test strip choice. (OEI; 04-13-00682; expected issue date: FY 2015)

Equipment and Supplies—Billing and Payments

Power mobility devices—Supplier compliance with payment requirements

We will review Medicare Part B payments for suppliers of PMDs to determine whether such payments were in accordance with Medicare requirements. We will focus particularly on whether PMDs are medically necessary and whether Medicare payments for PMD claims submitted by medical equipment suppliers are supported in accordance with requirements at 42 CFR § 410.38. (OAS; W-00-14-35703; various reviews; expected issue date: FY 2015)

Power mobility devices—Add-on payment for face-to-face examination

We will review Medicare Part B payments for PMDs to determine whether the Medicare requirements for a face-to-face examination were met. Medicare requires that the treating physician, when prescribing a PMD, conduct a face-to-face examination to determine the medical necessity of the PMD and write a prescription for the PMD. (42 CFR § 410.38(c)(2).) To receive compensation for conducting the face-to-face examination, the prescribing physician can bill for an E/M service and has the option of billing Medicare for an add-on payment for the sole purpose of documenting the need for the PMD. Prior OIG work found that when the prescribing physician did not bill the code for the add-on payment in addition to the E/M code, the resulting PMD claim was likely to be unallowable. (OAS; W-00-14-35460; expected issue date: FY 2015)

Lower limb prosthetics—Supplier compliance with payment requirements

We will review Medicare Part B payments for claims submitted by medical equipment suppliers for lower limb prosthetics to determine whether the requirements of CMS's *Benefit Policy Manual*, Pub. No. 100-02, ch. 15, § 120, were met. A national OIG review of suppliers of lower limb prosthetics identified 267 suppliers that had questionable billing. Earlier OIG work found that suppliers frequently submitted claims that did not meet certain Medicare requirements; were for beneficiaries with no claims from their referring physicians; and had other questionable billing characteristics (e.g., billing for lower limb prostheses for a high percentage of beneficiaries with no history of amputations or missing limbs). Such claims are questionable and, if determined to be improper, should not be paid by Medicare. Payments to service providers are precluded unless the provider has and furnishes upon request the information necessary to determine the amounts due. (Social Security Act, §1833(e).) Medicare does not pay for items or services that are not "reasonable and necessary." (Social Security Act, § 1862(a)(1)(A).) (OAS; W-00-13-35702; W-00-14-35702; various reviews; expected issue date: FY 2015)

Nebulizer machines and related drugs—Supplier compliance with payment requirements

We will review Medicare Part B payments for nebulizer machines and related drugs to determine whether medical equipment suppliers' claims for nebulizers and related drugs are medically necessary and are supported in accordance with Medicare requirements. Prior OIG work found that suppliers were overpaid approximately $46 million for inhalation drugs used with nebulizer machines. Medicare requires that such items be "reasonable and necessary." (Social Security Act § 1862(a)(1)(A).) Further, the local coverage determinations (LCDs) issued by the four Medicare contractors that process medical equipment and supply claims contain utilization guidelines and documentation requirements. (OAS; W-00-14-35465; W-00-15-35465; expected issue date: FY 2015)

➤ Frequently replaced supplies—Supplier compliance with medical necessity, frequency, and other requirements

We will review claims for frequently replaced medical equipment supplies to determine whether medical necessity, frequency, and other Medicare requirements are met. Prior OIG work found that suppliers automatically shipped continuous positive airway pressure system and respiratory-assist device supplies when no physician orders for refills were in effect. Such claims are improper and should not be submitted to Medicare for payment. For supplies and accessories used periodically, orders or certificates of medical necessity must specify the type of supplies needed and the frequency with which they must be replaced, used, or consumed. (CMS's *Medicare Program Integrity Manual*, Pub. 100-08, ch. 5, §§ 2.3 and 5.9.) Beneficiaries or their caregivers must specifically request refills of repetitive services and/or supplies before suppliers dispense them. (CMS's, *Medicare Claims Processing Manual*, Pub. 100-04, ch. 20, § 200.) Suppliers may not initiate refills of orders, and suppliers must not automatically dispense a quantity of supplies on a predetermined regular basis. Medicare does not pay for items or services that are not "reasonable and necessary." (Social Security Act, § 1862(a)(1)(A).) (OAS; W-00-15-35420; various reviews; expected issue date: FY 2015)

➤ Diabetes testing supplies—Supplier compliance with payment requirements for blood glucose test strips and lancets

We will review Medicare Part B payments for home blood glucose test strips and lancet supplies to determine their appropriateness. Prior OIG reviews determined that suppliers of diabetic-related supplies did not always comply with Federal requirements. As reflected in the LCDs issued by the Medicare contactors that process medical equipment and supply claims, physicians' orders for items billed to Medicare must include certain elements and be retained by the suppliers to support billing for the services. Suppliers of diabetes testing supplies are required to add a modifier code on the claim to identify when a patient is treated with insulin or not treated with insulin. The amount of supplies allowable for Medicare reimbursement differs depending on the applicable service code modifier. Medicare does not pay for items or services that are not "reasonable and necessary." (Social Security Act, § 1862(a)(1)(A).) (OAS; W-00-12-35407; W-00-14-35407; various reviews; expected issue date: FY 2015)

➤ Diabetes testing supplies—Effectiveness of system edits to prevent inappropriate payments for blood glucose test strips and lancets to multiple suppliers

We will review Medicare's claims processing edits (special system controls) designed to prevent payments to multiple suppliers of home blood glucose test strips and lancets and determine whether they are effective in preventing inappropriate payments. Prior OIG work found that inappropriate payments were made to multiple medical equipment suppliers for test strips and lancets dispensed to the same beneficiaries with overlapping service dates. The LCDs issued by the pertinent claims processing contractors state that medical equipment suppliers may not dispense test strips and lancets until beneficiaries have nearly exhausted the previously dispensed supplies. The LCDs also require that beneficiaries or their caregivers specifically request the refills before the suppliers dispense them. Medicare does not pay for items or services that are not "reasonable and necessary." (Social Security Act, § 1862(a)(1)(A).) (OAS; W-00-13-35604; W-00-14-35604; various reviews; expected issue date: FY 2015)

Other Providers and Suppliers

Acronyms and Abbreviations for Selected Terms:

ASC—ambulatory surgical center
CMS—Centers for Medicare & Medicaid Services
ESRD—end-stage renal disease

PHP—partial hospitalization program
PPS—prospective payment system
RHC—rural health clinic

Other Providers—Policies and Practices

➤ Ambulatory surgical centers—Payment system

We will review the appropriateness of Medicare's methodology for setting ambulatory surgical center (ASC) payment rates under the revised payment system. We will also determine whether a payment disparity exists between the ASC and hospital outpatient department payment rates for similar surgical procedures provided in both settings. A change in Federal law required the Secretary to implement a revised payment system for payment of surgical services furnished in ASCs beginning January 1, 2008. Accordingly, CMS implemented a revised ASC payment system modeled on the Outpatient Prospective Payment System. (Medicare Prescription Drug, Improvement, and Modernization Act of 2003 (MMA), § 626.) (See also 42 CFR § 416.171.) (OAS; W-00-13-35423; W-00-14-35423; various reviews; expected issue date: FY 2015)

➤ End-stage renal disease facilities—Payment system for renal dialysis services and drugs

We will review Medicare payments for and utilization of renal dialysis services and related drugs pursuant to the new bundled end-stage renal disease (ESRD) prospective payment system (PPS). We will compare facilities' acquisition costs for certain drugs to inflation-adjusted cost estimates and determine how costs for the drugs have changed. Previous OIG work found that data from the Bureau of Labor Statistics (BLS) did not accurately measure changes in facilities' acquisition costs for high-dollar ESRD drugs. However, CMS has based the ESRD PPS price updates on wage and price proxy data from BLS. Effective January 1, 2011, Federal law required CMS to begin implementation of a new system that bundles all costs related to ESRD care (including drugs that were previously separately billable) into a single per-treatment payment. (Social Security Act, § 1881(b)(14)(A)(i).) The bundled rate must be updated annually to reflect changes in the price of goods and services used in ESRD care. (75 Fed. Reg. 49030 at page 49151 (Aug. 12, 2010).) (OAS; W-00-14-35608; various reviews; expected issue date: FY 2015)

Other Providers—Billing and Payments

➤ Ambulance services—Questionable billing, medical necessity, and level of transport

We will examine Medicare claims data to assess the extent of questionable billing for ambulance services, such as transports that potentially never occurred or potentially were medically unnecessary transports to dialysis facilities. We will also determine whether Medicare payments for ambulance services were made in accordance with Medicare requirements. Prior OIG work found that Medicare made inappropriate payments for advanced life support emergency transports. Medicare pays for emergency and nonemergency ambulance services when a beneficiary's medical condition at the time of transport is such that other means of transportation are contraindicated (i.e., would endanger the beneficiary). (Social Security Act, § 1861(s)(7).) Medicare pays for different levels of ambulance service, including Basic Life Support and Advanced Life Support as well as specialty care transport. (42 CFR § 410.40(b).) (OEI; 09-12-00351; 09-12-00353; expected issue date: FY 2015; and OAS; W-00-11-35574; W-00-12-35574; W-00-13-35574; W-00-14-35574; various reviews; expected issue date: FY 2015)

➤ Ambulance services—Portfolio report on Medicare Part B payments

We will analyze and synthesize OIG evaluations, audits, investigations, and compliance guidance related to ground ambulance transport services paid by Medicare Part B to identify vulnerabilities, inefficiencies, and fraud trends and offer recommendations to improve detected vulnerabilities and minimize inappropriate payments for ambulance services. Prior OIG work identified fraud schemes and trends indicating overuse and medically unnecessary payments. The planned portfolio will offer recommendations to address the vulnerabilities that we have identified and improve efficiency. Medicare does not pay for items or services that are not "reasonable and necessary." (Social Security Act, § 1862(a)(1)(A).) Specifically, ambulance services are covered "where the use of other methods of transportation is contraindicated by the individual's condition...." (§ 1861(s)(7).) The *Medicare Benefit Policy Manual*, § 10.2.1, more specifically states that Medicare covers ambulance transports when a beneficiary's medical condition at the time of the transport is such that using other means of transportation would endanger the beneficiary's health. Coverage requirements and requirements for ambulance suppliers are in 42 CFR §§ 410.40 and 41. (OIG; OIG-12-14-02; expected issue date: FY 2016)

➤ Anesthesia services—Payments for personally performed services

We will review Medicare Part B claims for personally performed anesthesia services to determine whether they were supported in accordance with Medicare requirements. We will also determine whether Medicare payments for anesthesia services reported on a claim with the "AA" service code modifier met Medicare requirements. Physicians report the appropriate anesthesia modifier code to denote whether the service was personally performed or medically directed. (CMS, *Medicare Claims Processing Manual*, Pub. No. 100-04, ch. 12, § 50) Reporting an incorrect service code modifier on the claim as if services were personally performed by an anesthesiologist when they were not will result in Medicare's paying a higher amount. The service code "AA" modifier is used for anesthesia services personally performed by an anesthesiologist, whereas the QK modifier limits payment to 50 percent of the Medicare-allowed amount for personally performed services claimed with the AA modifier. Payments to any service provider are precluded unless the provider has furnished the information necessary to determine the amounts due. (Social Security Act, §1833(e).)

(OAS; W-00-13-35706; W-00-14-35706; W-00-15-35706; various reviews; expected issue date: FY 2015)

➤ Chiropractic services—Part B payments for noncovered services

We will review Medicare Part B payments for chiropractic services to determine whether such payments were claimed in accordance with Medicare requirements. Prior OIG work identified inappropriate payments for chiropractic services furnished during calendar year (CY) 2006. Subsequent OIG work (CY 2013) also identified unallowable Medicare payments for chiropractic services. Part B pays only for a chiropractor's manual manipulation of the spine to correct a subluxation if there is a neuro-musculoskeletal condition for which such manipulation is appropriate treatment. (42 CFR § 410.21(b).) Chiropractic maintenance therapy is not considered to be medically reasonable or necessary and is therefore not payable. (CMS's *Medicare Benefit Policy Manual*, Pub. No. 100-02, ch. 15, § 30.5B.) Medicare will not pay for items or services that are not "reasonable and necessary." (Social Security Act, § 1862(a)(1)(A).) (OAS; W-00-12-35606; W-00-13-35606; W-00-14-35606; various reviews; expected issue date: FY 2015)

➤ Chiropractic services—Questionable billing

We will determine and describe the extent of questionable billing for chiropractic services. Previous OIG work has demonstrated a history of vulnerabilities relative to inappropriate payments for chiropractic services, including recent work that identified a chiropractor with a 93-percent claim error rate and inappropriate Medicare payments of about $700,000. Although chiropractors may submit claims for any number of services, Medicare reimburses claims only for manual manipulations or treatment of subluxations of the spine that provides "a reasonable expectation of recovery or improvement of function." (CMS's *Medicare Benefit Policy Manual*, Pub. No. 100 02, ch. 15, § 240.1.3.) (OEI; 01-14-00200; expected issue date: FY 2015)

➤ Chiropractic services—Portfolio report on Medicare Part B payments

We will compile the results of prior OIG audits, evaluations, and investigations of chiropractic services paid by Medicare to identify trends in payment, compliance, and fraud vulnerabilities and offer recommendations to improve detected vulnerabilities. Prior OIG work identified inappropriate payments for chiropractic services that were medically unnecessary, were not documented in accordance with Medicare requirements, or were fraudulent. Medicare does not pay for items or services that are not "reasonable and necessary." (Social Security Act, § 1862(a)(1)(A).) Part B pays only for a chiropractor's manual manipulation of the spine to correct a subluxation if there is a neuro-musculoskeletal condition for which such manipulation is appropriate treatment. (42 CFR § 410.21(b).) CMS's *Medicare Benefit Policy Manual*, Pub. No. 100-02, ch. 15, § 30.5, states that chiropractic maintenance therapy is not considered to be medically reasonable or necessary and is therefore not payable. Further, § 240.1.2 of the manual establishes Medicare requirements for documenting chiropractic services. This planned work will offer recommendations to reduce Medicare chiropractic vulnerabilities detected in prior OIG work. (OAS; OIG-12-14-03; expected issue date: FY 2015)

➤ Diagnostic radiology—Medical necessity of high-cost tests

We will review Medicare payments for high-cost diagnostic radiology tests to determine whether the tests were medically necessary and to determine the extent to which use has increased for these tests. Medicare will not pay for items or services that are not "reasonable and necessary." (Social

Security Act, § 1862 (a)(1)(A).) (OAS; W-00-13-35454; W-00-14-35454; various reviews; expected issue date: FY 2015)

Imaging services—Payments for practice expenses

We will review Medicare Part B payments for imaging services to determine whether they reflect the expenses incurred and whether the utilization rates reflect industry practices. For selected imaging services, we will focus on the practice expense components, including the equipment utilization rate. Practice expenses may include office rent, wages, and equipment. Physicians are paid for services pursuant to the Medicare physician fee schedule, which covers the major categories of costs, including the physician professional cost component, malpractice insurance costs, and practice expenses. (Social Security Act, § 1848(c)(1)(B).) (OAS; W-00-13-35219; W-00-14-35219; various reviews; expected issue date: FY 2015)

Selected independent clinical laboratory billing requirements (new)

We will review Medicare payments to independent clinical laboratories to determine laboratories' compliance with selected billing requirements. We will use the results of these reviews to identify clinical laboratories that routinely submit improper claims and recommend recovery of overpayments. Prior OIG audits, investigations, and inspections have identified independent clinical laboratory areas at risk for noncompliance with Medicare billing requirements. Payments to service providers are precluded unless the provider has and furnishes upon request the information necessary to determine the amounts due. (Social Security Act, §1833(e).) We will focus on independent clinical laboratories with claims that may be at risk for overpayments. (OAS; W-00-14-35726; W-00-15-35726; various reviews; expected issue date: FY 2015)

Ophthalmologists—Inappropriate and questionable billing

We will review Medicare claims data to identify potentially inappropriate and questionable billing for ophthalmology services during 2012. We will also determine the locations and specialties of providers with questionable billing. Medicare payments for Part B physician services, which include ophthalmologists, are authorized by the Social Security Act, § 1832(a)(1), and 42 CFR § 410.20. In 2010, Medicare allowed more than $6.8 billion for services provided by ophthalmologists. (OEI; 04-12-00280; 04-12-00281; expected issue date: FY 2015)

Physicians—Place-of-service coding errors

We will review physicians' coding on Medicare Part B claims for services performed in ASCs and hospital outpatient departments to determine whether they properly coded the places of service. Prior OIG reviews determined that physicians did not always correctly code nonfacility places of service on Part B claims submitted to and paid by Medicare contractors. Federal regulations provide for different levels of payments to physicians depending on where services are performed. (42 CFR § 414.32.) Medicare pays a physician a higher amount when a service is performed in a nonfacility setting, such as a physician's office, than it does when the service is performed in a hospital outpatient department or, with certain exceptions, in an ASC. (OAS; W-00-13-35113; W-00-14-35113; various reviews; expected issue date: FY 2015)

Physical therapists—High use of outpatient physical therapy services

We will review outpatient physical therapy services provided by independent therapists to determine whether they were in compliance with Medicare reimbursement regulations. Prior OIG work found that claims for therapy services provided by independent physical therapists were not reasonable or were not properly documented or that the therapy services were not medically necessary. Our focus is on independent therapists who have a high utilization rate for outpatient physical therapy services. Medicare will not pay for items or services that are not "reasonable and necessary." (Social Security Act, § 1862(a)(1)(A).) Documentation requirements for therapy services are in CMS's *Medicare Benefit Policy Manual*, Pub. No. 100-02, ch. 15, § 220.3. (OAS; W-00-11-35220; W-00-12-35220; W-00-13-35220; W-00-14-35220; W-00-15-35220; various reviews; expected issue date: FY 2015)

Portable x-ray equipment—Supplier compliance with transportation and setup fee requirements

We will review Medicare payments for portable x-ray equipment services to determine whether payments were correct and were supported by documentation. We will also assess the qualifications of the technologists who performed the services. Prior OIG work found that Medicare may have improperly paid portable x-ray suppliers for return trips to nursing facilities (i.e., multiple trips to a facility in 1 day). Medicare generally reimburses for portable x-ray services if the conditions for coverage are met. (42 CFR §§ 486.100–486.110.) (OAS; W-00-14-35464; various reviews; expected issue date: FY 2015)

Sleep disorder clinics—High use of sleep-testing procedures

We will examine Medicare payments to physicians, hospital outpatient departments, and independent diagnostic testing facilities for sleep-testing procedures to assess the appropriateness of Medicare payments for high-use sleep-testing procedures and determine whether they were in accordance with Medicare requirements. An OIG analysis of CY 2010 Medicare payments for Current Procedural Terminology[1] codes 95810 and 95811, which totaled approximately $415 million, showed high utilization associated with these sleep-testing procedures. Medicare will not pay for items or services that are not "reasonable and necessary." (Social Security Act, § 1862(a)(1)(A).) To the extent that repeated diagnostic testing is performed on the same beneficiary and the prior test results are still pertinent, repeated tests may not be reasonable and necessary. Requirements for coverage of sleep tests under Part B are in CMS's *Medicare Benefit Policy Manual*, Pub. No. 100-02, ch. 15, § 70. (OAS; W-00-10-35521; W-00-12-35521; W-00-13-35521; W-00-14-35521; various reviews; expected issue date: FY 2015)

---

[1] The five character codes and descriptions included in this document are obtained from Current Procedural Terminology (CPT®), copyright [2011] by the American Medical Association (AMA). CPT is developed by the AMA as a listing of descriptive terms and five character identifying codes and modifiers for reporting medical services and procedures. Any use of CPT outside of this document should refer to the most current version of the Current Procedural Terminology available from AMA. Applicable FARS/DFARS apply.

Prescription Drugs

Acronyms and Abbreviations for Selected Terms Used in This Section:

AMP—average manufacturer price
ASP—average sales price
CMS—Centers for Medicare & Medicaid Services

FDA—Food and Drug Administration
LCD—local coverage determination
MAC—Medicare Administrative Contractor

Prescription Drugs—Policies and Practices

> ### Comparison of average sales prices to average manufacturer prices

We will review Medicare Part B drug prices by comparing average sales prices (ASPs) to average manufacturer prices (AMPs) and identify drug prices that exceed a designated threshold. In 2005, Medicare began paying for most Part B drugs using a new methodology based on the ASP. The enabling law required that OIG compare ASPs with AMPs. (Social Security Act, § 1847A(d)(2)(B).) Pursuant to the requirement, OIG conducts such reviews and issues quarterly and annual reports of its findings. When OIG finds that the ASP for a drug exceeds the AMP by a certain percentage (5 percent), OIG notifies the Secretary, who may disregard the ASP for the drug when setting reimbursement amounts (e.g., apply a price substitution policy). (OEI; 03-14-00520; various studies; expected issue date: FY 2015)

> ### Part B payments for drugs purchased under the 340B Program

We will determine how much Medicare Part B spending could be reduced if Medicare were able to share in the savings for 340B-purchased drugs. We will calculate the amount by which ASP-based payments exceed 340B prices and estimate potential savings on the basis of various shared-benefit methodologies. Previous OIG work revealed that some Medicaid State agencies have developed strategies to take advantage of the discounts on 340B drugs. The 340B Program requires drug manufacturers to provide discounted outpatient drugs to approximately 10,000 covered entities, including tribal health centers, children's hospitals, and tuberculosis clinics. Medicare Part B reimburses for almost all covered outpatient drugs (including those purchased by 340B entities) on the basis of the ASP, regardless of the amount paid for the drug. Medicare Part B providers that purchase drugs under the 340B program can fully retain the difference between the ASP-based payment amount and the 340B purchase price. (OEI; 12-14-00030; expected issue date: FY 2015)

Prescription Drugs—Billing and Payments

> ### Payments for immunosuppressive drug claims with KX modifiers

We will determine whether Part B payments for immunosuppressive drugs that were billed with a service code modifier "KX" met Medicare documentation requirements. Medicare claims for immunosuppressive drugs reported with the KX modifier may not always meet documentation requirements for payment under Part B. Medicare Part B covers Food and Drug Administration (FDA)-approved immunosuppressive drugs and drugs used in immunosuppressive therapy when a beneficiary receives an organ transplant for which immunosuppressive therapy is appropriate. (Social Security Act, § 1861(s).) Since July 2008, suppliers that furnish an immunosuppressive drug to a Medicare beneficiary annotate the Medicare claim with the KX modifier to signify that the supplier retains documentation of the beneficiary's transplant date and that such transplant date preceded the date of service for furnishing the drug. (CMS's *Medicare Claims Processing Manual*, Pub. No. 100 04, ch. 17, § 80.3.) (OAS; W-00-14-35707; W-00-15-35707; various reviews; expected issue date: FY 2015)

➢ Payments for outpatient drugs and administration of the drugs

We will review Medicare outpatient payments to providers for certain drugs (e.g., chemotherapy drugs) and the administration of the drugs to determine whether Medicare overpaid providers because of incorrect coding or overbilling of units. Prior OIG reviews have identified certain drugs, particularly chemotherapy drugs, as vulnerable to incorrect coding. Providers must bill accurately and completely for services provided. (CMS's *Claims Processing Manual*, Pub. No. 100-04, ch. 1, §§ 70.2.3.1 and 80.3.2.2.) Further, providers must report units of service as the number of times that a service or procedure was performed. (Chapter 5, § 20.2, and ch. 26, § 10.4.) (OAS; W-00-12-35576; W-00-13-35576; W-00-14-35576; various reviews; expected issue date: FY 2015)

Prescription Drugs—Quality of Care and Safety

➢ Covered uses for Medicare Part B drugs

We will review the oversight actions that CMS and its claims processing contractors take to ensure that payments for Part B drugs meet the appropriate coverage criteria. We will also identify challenges contractors face when making coverage decisions for drugs. If Part B MACs do not have effective oversight mechanisms, Medicare and its beneficiaries may pay for drugs with little clinical evidence of the drugs' safety and effectiveness. Medicare Part B generally covers drugs when they are used to treat conditions approved by FDA, referred to as "on-label" uses. Part B may also cover drugs when an "off-label" use of the drug is supported in major drug compendia or when an off-label use is supported by clinical evidence in authoritative medical literature. (*Medicare Benefit Policy Manual*, Pub. No. 100-02, ch. 15, § 50.4.2.) (OEI; 03-13-00450; expected issue date: FY 2015)

➢ Ethics—Conflicts of interest involving prescription drug compendia

We will determine the extent to which publishers of authoritative prescription drug compendia recognized by CMS have publicly transparent processes for evaluating anticancer drug therapies and identifying conflicts of interest related to the therapies included in the compendia. Generally, Medicare covers drugs that are approved by FDA and supported by one or more drug compendia recognized by CMS. (CMS's *Medicare Benefit Policy Manual*, Pub. No. 100-02, ch. 1, § 30, and ch. 15, § 50.) Recent concerns have highlighted the issue of conflicts of interest involving the drug compendia; however, CMS does not generally require the compendia to publish conflict information, and it is unclear whether CMS conducts any oversight of the strength of the compendias' policies or the nature of their conflicts. Since 2010, publishers must have publicly transparent processes for evaluating anticancer drug therapies and for identifying potential conflicts related to inclusion of those therapies in the compendia (Social Security Act, § 1861). (OEI; 07-13-00220; expected issue date: FY 2015)

Part A and Part B Contractors

Acronyms and Abbreviations for Selected Terms:

CMS—Centers for Medicare & Medicaid Services
FAR—Federal Acquisition Regulation

PSC—Program Safeguard Contractor
ZPIC—Zone Program Integrity Contractor

Oversight of Contracts

➤ Contract management at the Centers for Medicare & Medicaid Services

We will determine the number, types, and contract value of currently active contracts administered under the Federal Acquisition Regulation (FAR) by CMS. We also will determine the number and total value of FAR contracts that CMS has not closed out as required under FAR and will identify CMS's barriers to managing and closing of FAR contracts. CMS relies extensively on contractors to help it carry out its basic mission, including administration, management, and oversight of its health programs. In FY 2013, CMS obligated $5.4 billion under contracts for a variety of goods and services. Previous Government Accountability Office (GAO) reports highlighted the vulnerabilities and weaknesses in the contracting environment at CMS, including problems with the contract closeout process. Given the number of contracts and the obligated dollars, oversight and monitoring are vital for ensuring effective programs and safeguarding taxpayer dollars. In addition, timely and effective contract closeouts protect the Government's financial interests and allow for recovery of excess funds. (OEI; 03-12-00680; various expected issue date: FY 2015)

➤ Administrative costs claimed by Medicare contractors

We will review administrative costs claimed by various contractors for their Medicare activities, focusing on costs claimed by terminated contractors. We will also determine whether the costs claimed were reasonable, allocable, and allowable. We will coordinate with CMS regarding the selection of the contractors we will review. Criteria include Appendix B of the Medicare contract with CMS and the FAR at 48 CFR Part 31. (OAS; W-00-13-35005; W-00-14-35005; various reviews; expected issue date: FY 2015)

➤ Executive compensation benchmark

We will review contractor employee salaries charged to Medicare to determine whether the selected contractors applied a senior executive compensation benchmark required by regulation, and we will determine the potential cost savings if contractors were required to apply the same benchmark to all employee compensation. Costs incurred after January 1, 1998, for compensation of a senior executive in excess of the benchmark compensation amount determined applicable for the contractor fiscal year by the Administrator, Office of Federal Procurement Policy (OFPP), under section 39 of the OFPP Act (41 U.S.C. 435) are unallowable. (48 CFR § 31.205-6(p).) We will determine the potential effect of expanding the executive compensation benchmark to all employees. The term "senior executive" is defined as the top five compensated employees of each organizational segment. (48 CFR § 31.205-6(p)(4)(B)(ii).) The issue of high salaries for executives of Government contractors has been examined in the news media. (OAS; W-00-13-35710; various reviews; expected issue date: FY 2015)

Contractor pension cost requirements

We will determine whether Medicare contractors have calculated and claimed reimbursement for Medicare's share of various employee pension costs in accordance with their Medicare contracts and applicable Federal requirements. We will determine whether contractors have fully implemented contract clauses requiring them to determine and separately account for the employee pension assets and liabilities allocable to their contracts with Medicare. We will also review Medicare carriers and fiscal intermediaries (FIs) whose Medicare contracts have been terminated, assess Medicare's share of future pension costs, and determine the amount of excess pension assets as of the closing dates. Applicable requirements are found in the FAR at 48 CFR Subpart 31.2; Cost Accounting Standards (CAS) 412 and 413; and the Medicare contract, Appendix B, § XVI. (OAS; W-00-14-35067; W-00-14-35094; various reviews; expected issue date: FY 2015)

Contractor postretirement benefits and supplemental employee retirement plan costs

We will review the postretirement health benefit costs and the supplemental employee retirement plans of Medicare FIs and carriers to determine the allowability, allocability, and reasonableness of the benefits and plans, as well as the costs charged to Medicare contracts. Criteria are in the FAR at 48 CFR §§ 31.201 through 31.205. (OAS; W-00-13-35095; W-00-14-35095; various reviews; expected issue date: FY 2015)

Contractor Functions and Performance

Medicare benefit integrity contractors' activities

We will review and report the level of benefit integrity activity performed by Medicare benefit integrity contractors in CYs 2012 and 2013. CMS contracts with entities to carry out benefit integrity activities to safeguard the Medicare program against fraud, waste, and abuse. Activities that these contractors perform include analyzing data to identify aberrant billing patterns, conducting fraud investigations, responding to requests for information from law enforcement, and referring suspected cases of fraud to law enforcement for prosecution. Program Safeguard Contractors (PSCs) and Zone Program Integrity Contractors (ZPICs) carry out benefit integrity activities for Medicare Parts A and B, and a Medicare Drug Integrity Contractor (MEDIC) carries out benefit integrity activities for Medicare Parts C and D. (OEI; 03-13-00620; expected issue date: FY 2015)

ZPICs and PSCs—Identification and collection status of Medicare overpayments

We will determine the total amount of overpayments that ZPICs and PSCs identified and referred to claims processors in 2013 and the amount of these overpayments that claims processors collected. We will also review the procedures for tracking collections on overpayments identified by ZPICs and PSCs. OIG has issued several reports regarding the tracking and collection of the overpayments that Medicare's contractors have made to providers. In response, CMS stated that it has added reporting requirements that would improve overpayment tracking among the claims processors and ZPICs and PSCs. ZPICs and PSCs are required to detect and deter fraud and abuse in Medicare Part A and/or Part B in their jurisdictions. They conduct investigations; refer cases to law enforcement; and take administrative actions, such as referring overpayments to claims processors for collection and return to the Medicare program. (OEI; 03-13-00630; expected issue date: FY 2015)

Information Technology Security, Protected Health Information, and Data Accuracy

➢ Medicare contractor information systems security programs—Annual report to Congress

We will review independent evaluations of information systems security programs of Medicare FIs, carriers, and MACs. We will report to Congress on our assessment of the scope and sufficiency of the independent evaluations and summarize their results. Federal law requires independent evaluations of the security programs of FIs, carriers, and MACs and requires OIG to assess such evaluations and report the results of its assessments to Congress. (MMA, § 912.) (OAS; W-00-14-41010; W-00-15-41010; expected issue date: FY 2015)

➢ Controls over networked medical devices at hospitals

We will examine whether CMS oversight of hospitals' security controls over networked medical devices is sufficient to effectively protect associated electronic protected health information (ePHI) and ensure beneficiary safety. Computerized medical devices, such as dialysis machines, radiology systems, and medication dispensing systems that are integrated with electronic medical records (EMRs) and the larger health network, pose a growing threat to the security and privacy of personal health information. Such medical devices use hardware, software, and networks to monitor a patient's medical status and transmit and receive related data using wired or wireless communications. To participate in Medicare, providers such as hospitals are required to secure medical records and patient information, including ePHI. (42 CFR § 482.24(b).) Medical device manufacturers provide Manufacturer Disclosure Statement for Medical Device Security (MDS2) forms to assist health care providers in assessing the vulnerability and risks associated with ePHI that is transmitted or maintained by a medical device. (OAS; W-00-15-42020; various reviews; expected issue date: FY 2015)

Other Part A and Part B Program Management Issues

Provider Eligibility

➢ Enhanced enrollment screening process for Medicare providers

We will determine the extent to which and the way in which CMS and its contractors have implemented enhanced screening procedures for Medicare providers pursuant to the ACA, § 6401. We will also collect data on and report the number of initial enrollments and enrollment revalidations approved and denied by CMS before and after the implementation of the enhanced screening procedures. As part of an effort to prevent fraud, waste, and abuse resulting from vulnerabilities in the Medicare enrollment process, CMS is implementing new authorities that include site visits, fingerprinting, and background checks, as well as an automated provider screening process. (OEI; 03-13-00050; expected issue date: FY 2015; ACA.)

New Models

➤ Risk Assessment of CMS' Administration of the Pioneer Accountable Care Organization Model (new)

We will conduct a risk assessment of the Pioneer Accountable Care Organization (ACO) Model. An ACO is a group of providers and suppliers of services (e.g., hospitals and physicians and others involved in patient care) that will work together to coordinate care for the Medicare fee-for-service beneficiaries they serve. The Centers for Medicare & Medicaid Innovation was created to test innovative care and service delivery models and is administering the Pioneer ACO Model. (ACA, § 3021.) We will conduct a risk assessment of internal controls over administration of the Pioneer ACO Model. (OAS; W-00-00-00000; expected issue date: FY 2015; ACA)

Medicare Part C and Part D

Beneficiaries must be enrolled in both Part A and Part B to join one of the Part C Medicare Advantage (MA) plans, which are administered by MA organizations. MA organizations are public or private organizations licensed by States as risk-bearing entities under contract with the Centers for Medicare & Medicaid Services (CMS) to provide covered services. MA organizations may offer one or more plans. Medicare's optional outpatient prescription drug benefit, known as Medicare Part D, took effect on January 1, 2006. (Medicare Prescription Drug, Improvement, and Modernization Act of 2003 (MMA).) Part D is a voluntary benefit available to Medicare beneficiaries.

Acronyms and Abbreviations for Selected Terms:

CMS—Centers for Medicare & Medicaid Services   PDE—prescription drug event
MA—Medicare Advantage

Part C – Medicare Advantage

MA plans provide all Part A and Part B services and generally provide additional services not covered by traditional Medicare. Beneficiaries usually pay monthly premiums and copayments that are often less than the coinsurance and deductibles under the original Medicare Part A and Part B. In most cases, these plans also offer Part D prescription drug coverage. Costs and benefits vary by plan.

Efforts for FY 2015 and beyond may include additional work examining the soundness of rates and risk and payment adjustments in the MA Program.

MA Organizations' Compliance With Part C Requirements

➢ Encounter data—CMS oversight of data integrity

We will review the extent to which MA encounter data reflecting the items and services provided to MA plan enrollees are complete and consistent and are verified for accuracy by CMS. Prior CMS and Office of Inspector General (OIG) audits indicated vulnerabilities in the accuracy of risk adjustment data reporting by MA organizations. In 2012, MA encounter data reporting requirements were expanded from an abbreviated set of primary diagnosis data to a more comprehensive set of data. (CMS's *One Time Notification*, Pub. 100-20, CR 7562.) (OEI; 00-00-00000; expected issue date: FY 2016)

➢ Risk adjustment data—Sufficiency of documentation supporting diagnoses

We will review the medical record documentation to ensure that it supports the diagnoses MA organizations submitted to CMS for use in CMS's risk-score calculations and determine whether the diagnoses submitted complied with Federal requirements. Prior OIG reviews have shown that medical record documentation does not always support the diagnoses submitted to CMS by MA organizations. MA organizations are required to submit risk adjustment data to CMS in accordance with CMS instructions. (42 CFR § 422.310(b).) Payments to MA organizations are adjusted on the basis of the health status of each beneficiary, so inaccurate diagnoses may cause CMS to pay MA organizations improper amounts. (Social Security Act, §§ 1853(a)(1)(C) and (a)(3).) (OAS; W-00-14-35078; W-00-15-35078; various reviews; expected issue date: FY 2015)

Part D – Prescription Drug Program

The administration of Part D depends upon extensive coordination and information sharing among Federal and State Government agencies, drug plan sponsors, contractors, health care providers, and third-party payers. CMS and drug plan sponsors share responsibility for protecting the Part D program from fraud, waste, and abuse. Payments to drug plan sponsors, made on the basis of bids, risk adjustments, and reconciliations, add to the complexities and challenges of the benefit.

CMS provides prescription drug coverage for over 37 million Medicare beneficiaries through Part D. In 2012, Medicare Part D expenditures totaled almost $67 billion. Ensuring the appropriate use of prescription drugs in Medicare is vital for financial reasons as well as patient safety and quality of care. Future OIG work planning efforts for fiscal year (FY) 2015 and beyond will consider prescribing policies and practices and the efficacy of safeguards intended to protect beneficiaries and the programs from drug overutilization and improper payments.

Medicare, Sponsor, and Manufacturer Policies and Practices

➢ Savings potential of adjusting risk corridors

We will analyze risk-sharing payments between Medicare and Part D sponsors to determine whether cost savings could have been realized had the existing risk corridor thresholds remained at 2006 and 2007 levels. CMS has the authority to retain existing risk corridor thresholds or widen them for plan year 2012 and beyond. Risk corridors determine the amount of unexpected profits or losses that Medicare and sponsors share. (Social Security Act § 1860D-15.) (OEI; 02-14-00320; expected issue date: FY 2015)

Sponsor Compliance With Part D Requirements

➢ Documentation of administrative costs in sponsors' bid proposals

We will review the sufficiency of Part D sponsors' documentation supporting the administrative costs they included in their annual bid proposals to CMS. Part D sponsors submit bids for the costs of providing prescription drug coverage, including administrative costs. (Social Security Act, § 1860D-11(b) and 42 CFR § 423.265(c)(1).) Medicare's subsidy payments to Part D plans and beneficiary premiums are calculated on the basis of the sponsors' bids. (OAS; W-00-14-35506; various reviews; expected issue date: FY 2015)

➤ Reconciliation of payments—Sponsor reporting of direct and indirect remuneration

We will determine whether Part D sponsors complied with Medicare requirements for reporting direct and indirect remunerations (DIR). Medicare calculates certain payments to sponsors on the basis of amounts actually paid by the Part D sponsors, net of DIR. (42 CFR pt. 423, subpart G.) DIR includes all rebates, subsidies, and other price concessions from sources (including, but not limited to, manufacturers and pharmacies) that serve to decrease the costs incurred by Part D sponsors for Part D drugs. CMS requires that Part D sponsors submit DIR reports for use in the payment reconciliation process. (OAS; W-00-13-35508; W-00-14-35508; various reviews; expected issue date: FY 2015)

➤ Reconciliation of payments—Reopening final payment determinations

We will review CMS policies, procedures, instructions, and processes for reopening final payment determinations and determine the adequacy of Part D sponsor compliance and sponsor-submitted data. CMS may reopen and revise an initial or reconsidered final payment determination within time limitations that apply, depending on the reason for reopening. (42 CFR § 423.346(a).) In April 2013, CMS announced that it planned to reopen 2007 and 2008 reconciliations during the 2013 calendar year and would assess at a later time whether it is necessary to reopen 2009, 2010, and 2011 reconciliations. CMS allowed sponsors to request reopening and to submit additional prescription drug event (PDE) data and DIR data. (OAS; W-00-14-35621; W-00-15-35621; various reviews; expected issue date: FY 2015)

➤ Ensuring dual eligibles' access to drugs under Part D

We will review the extent to which drug formularies developed by Part D sponsors include drugs commonly used by dual-eligible beneficiaries, as required. Dual-eligible beneficiaries are enrolled in Medicaid but qualify for prescription drug coverage under Medicare Part D. As long as Part D plans meet certain limitations outlined in 42 CFR § 423.120, they have discretion to include different Part D drugs and drug utilization tools in their formularies. The Patient Protection and Affordable Care Act (ACA), § 3313, requires OIG to conduct this review annually. (OEI; 00-00-0000; expected issue date: FY 2015; ACA)

➤ Recommendation followup: Oversight of conflicts of interest in Medicare prescription drug decisions (new)

We will determine what steps CMS has taken to improve its oversight of Part D sponsors' Pharmacy and Therapeutics (P&T) committee conflict-of-interest procedures. Federal law and regulations require Medicare Part D P&T committees to make prescription drug coverage decisions on the basis of scientific evidence and standards of practice. To comply with the law, Part D sponsors' P&T committees must prevent conflicts of interest from influencing members to give preference to certain drugs. The OIG report, *Gaps in Oversight of Conflicts of Interest in Medicare Prescription Drug Decisions* (OEI-05-10-00450), found that CMS does not adequately oversee Part D sponsors' P&T committee compliance with Federal conflict-of-interest requirements. (OEI; 00-00-00000; expected issue date: FY 2015)

Part D Billing and Payments

➢ Documentation of pharmacies' prescription drug event data

We will conduct additional reviews of selected retail pharmacies identified in a prior OIG report as having questionable Part D billing. We will determine whether Medicare Part D PDE records submitted by the selected pharmacies were adequately supported and complied with applicable Federal requirements. Drug plan sponsors must submit the information necessary for the Secretary to determine payments to the plans. (Social Security Act, § 1860D-15(f)(1).) (OAS; W-00-13-35411; various reviews; expected issue date: FY 2015)

➢ Medicare payments for HIV drugs for deceased beneficiaries

We will determine the extent to which Medicare Part D paid for human immunodeficiency virus (HIV) drugs for deceased beneficiaries in 2012. Part D covers drugs that are prescribed and used for medically accepted indications. Drugs dispensed for deceased beneficiaries do not meet Medicare Part D coverage requirements. (OEI; 02-11-00172; expected issue date: FY 2015)

➢ Quality of sponsor data used in calculating coverage-gap discounts

We will review data submitted by Part D sponsors for use in calculating the coverage gap discount to assess the accuracy of the data and determine whether beneficiary payments are correct and amounts paid to sponsors are supported. The ACA required the Secretary to establish a Medicare coverage-gap discount program to provide relief to beneficiaries who are responsible for paying all drug costs during their coverage gaps. (Social Security Act, § 1860D-14A, as amended by the ACA, § 3301.) Sponsors track beneficiary payment information and the drug cost data necessary to calculate eligibility for the program. (OAS; W-00-14-35611; various reviews; expected issue date: FY 2015; ACA)

Medicaid Program

The Federal Government and States jointly fund Medicaid, a program that provides medical assistance to certain low-income individuals. The Federal share of a State's expenditures is called the Federal medical assistance percentage (FMAP). States have considerable flexibility in structuring their Medicaid programs within broad Federal guidelines governing eligibility, provider payment levels, and benefits. As a result, Medicaid programs vary widely from State to State. Many States contract with managed care organizations (MCOs) to provide or coordinate comprehensive health services.

Protecting an expanding Medicaid program from fraud, waste, and abuse takes on a heightened urgency as the program continues to grow in spending and in the number of people it serves. Our continuing and new reviews of Medicaid in fiscal year (FY) 2015 address: prescription drugs; billing, payment, reimbursement, quality, and safety of home health services, community-based care, and other services, equipment, and supplies; State management of Medicaid, information system controls and security, and Medicaid managed care.

Planning for FY 2015 and beyond may include examinations of beneficiary eligibility determinations and FMAP assignments, data and methodologies used to ensure program integrity, and inefficient payment policies or practices—targeting areas prone to payment errors. Going forward, OIG expects to expand its portfolio examining protections to ensure quality of care and access to services, as well as work examining drug diversion and abuse.

Medicaid Prescription Drug Reviews

Acronyms and Abbreviations for Selected Terms:

AMP—average manufacturer price
CMS—Centers for Medicare & Medicaid Services

DUR—drug utilization review
MCO—managed care organization

State and Manufacturer Compliance With Medicaid Requirements

➤ States' use of Medicaid drug utilization review to reduce the inappropriate dispensing of opioids

We will review the education and enforcement actions that States have taken on the basis of information generated by their drug utilization review (DUR) programs related to inappropriate dispensing and potential abuse of prescription opiates. We also will review State oversight of MCOs' DUR programs and any resulting actions related to inappropriate dispensing of opiates. States are required to establish DUR programs to receive the Federal share of Medicaid payments. (42 CFR § 456.703.) DUR involves, among other functions, ongoing and periodic examination of claims data to identify patterns of fraud, abuse, gross overuse, or medically unnecessary care and implementing corrective action when needed. (OEI; 05-13-00550; expected issue date: FY 2015)

➢ Manufacturer compliance with AMP reporting requirements

We will determine whether manufacturer compliance with average manufacturer price (AMP) reporting requirements has changed since 2008 and identify actions that the Centers for Medicare & Medicaid Services (CMS) has taken to improve compliance with AMP reporting requirements. Manufacturer-reported AMPs play a critical role in Federal cost containment strategies for prescription drugs. Price-reporting obligations for certain drug manufacturers, including the obligation to report AMP data to CMS quarterly and monthly, are set forth in the Social Security Act, § 1927(b)(3), and 42 CFR §§ 447.510(a) and (d). A previous OIG review found that, in 2008, more than half of the drug manufacturers that were required to submit quarterly AMPs to CMS failed to comply with reporting requirements in at least one quarter. Manufacturers were even less likely to comply with monthly AMP reporting requirements. (OEI; 03-14-00150; expected issue date: FY 2015)

➢ States collection of rebates on physician-administered drugs

We will determine whether States have established adequate accountability and internal controls for collecting Medicaid rebates on physician-administered drugs. We will assess States' processes for collecting national drug code information on claims for physician-administered drugs and subsequent processes for billing and collecting rebates. Prior OIG work identified concerns with States' collection and submission of data to CMS, including national drug codes that identify drug manufacturers, thus allowing States to invoice the manufacturers responsible for paying rebates. (Deficit Reduction Act of 2005 (DRA).) To be eligible for Federal matching funds, States are required to collect rebates on covered outpatient drugs administered by physicians. (Social Security Act, § 1927(a).) (OAS; W-00-12-31400; W-00-13-31400; W-00-14-31400; various reviews; expected issue date: FY 2015)

➢ State collection of rebates for drugs dispensed to Medicaid MCO enrollees (new)

We will determine whether the States are collecting prescription drug rebates from pharmaceutical manufacturers for Medicaid MCOs. Drugs dispensed by Medicaid MCOs were excluded from this requirement until March 23, 2010. Section 2501 (c) of the Patient Protection and Affordable Care Act (ACA) expanded the rebate requirement to include drugs dispensed to MCO enrollees. Medicaid MCOs are required to report enrollees' drug utilization to the State for the purpose of collecting rebates from manufacturers. (OAS; W-00-14-31483; W-00-15-31483; various reviews; expected issue date: FY 2015; ACA)

➢ States' collection and reporting of rebates

We will determine the amount of offset rebates (i.e., the amount of drug manufacturer rebates attributed to the increase in Medicaid rebates under the ACA) reported by States. We will also determine the amount of supplemental drug rebates that States collected during a selected period. The ACA, § 2501, increased the basic Federal minimum rebate amount that helps lower the costs of Medicaid prescription drug programs. (OEI; 03-12-00520; expected issue date: FY 2015; work in progress; ACA)

> ## Comparison of Medicare Part D and Medicaid pharmacy reimbursement and rebates

This review, which is a followup to previous work, will compare pharmacy reimbursement and rebate amounts for a sample of brand-name drugs paid for by Medicare Part D and by Medicaid, taking into account changes to Medicaid rebates under the ACA. Manufacturer rebates reduce drug expenditures under both Medicare Part D and Medicaid. A previous OIG review revealed that Part D sponsors and State Medicaid agencies paid pharmacies roughly the same amounts for brand-name drugs. However, statutorily defined Medicaid unit rebate amounts for brand-name drugs exceeded Part D unit rebate amounts by a substantial margin, resulting in lower drug program costs for Medicaid. (OEI; 03-13-00650; expected issue date: FY 2015; ACA)

State Claims for Federal Reimbursement

> ## Medicaid payments for multiuse vials of Herceptin

We will review States' claims for the Federal share of Medicaid payments for the drug Herceptin, which is used to treat breast cancer, to determine whether providers properly billed the States for the drug. We will determine whether providers' claims to States were complete and accurate and were billed in accordance with the regulations of the selected States. Prior OIG audits of Herceptin have shown provider noncompliance with Medicare billing requirements. Similar issues may occur in Medicaid. (OAS; W-00-14-31476; various reviews; expected issue date: FY 2015)

Home Health Services and Other Community-Based Care

Acronyms and Abbreviations for Selected Terms Used in This Section:

CDT—continuing day treatment
CMS—Centers for Medicare & Medicaid Services

HCBS—home and community-based services
HHA—home health agency

Billing and Payments

> ## Adult day health care services

We will review Medicaid payments by States for adult day care services to determine whether providers complied with Federal and State requirements. Adult day health care programs provide health, therapeutic, and social services and activities to program enrollees. Beneficiaries enrolled must meet eligibility requirements, and services must be furnished in accordance with a plan of care. Medicaid allows payments for adult day health care through various authorities, including home and community-based services (HCBS) waivers. (Social Security Act, § 1915, and 42 CFR § 440.180.) Prior OIG work shows that these payments do not always comply with State and Federal requirements. (OAS; W-00-12-31386; W-00-13-31386; various reviews; expected issue date: FY 2015)

> Continuing day treatment mental health services

We will review Medicaid payments to continuing day treatment (CDT) mental health services providers to determine whether their claims were adequately supported. Our review will follow up on a State Commission's findings of unsubstantiated claims. CDT providers render an array of services to people with mental illnesses. CDT providers bill Medicaid on the basis of the number of service hours rendered to beneficiaries. One State's regulations require that a billing for a visit/service hour be supported by documentation indicating the nature and extent of services provided. A State commission found that more than 50 percent of the service hours billed by CDT providers in that State could not be substantiated. To be allowable, costs must be authorized, or not prohibited, under State or local laws or regulations. (Office of Management and Budget (OMB) Circular A-87, *Cost Principles for State, Local, and Indian Tribal Governments*, Att. A, § C.1.c.) (OAS; W-00-13-31128; W-00-14-31128; various reviews; expected issue date: FY 2015)

State Claims for Federal Reimbursement

> Room and board costs associated with HCBS waiver program payments

We will determine whether selected States claimed Federal reimbursement for unallowable room and board costs associated with services provided under the terms and conditions of HCBS waiver programs. We will determine whether HCBS payments included the costs of room and board and identify the methods the States used to determine the amounts paid. Medicaid covers the cost of HCBS provided under a written plan of care to individuals in need of such services but does not allow for payment of room and board costs. (42 CFR §§ 441.301(b) and 441.310(a).) HCBS are provided pursuant to the Social Security Act, § 1915(c). States may use various methods to pay for such services, such as a settlement process based on annual cost reports or prospective rates with rate adjustments based on cost report data and cost-trending factors. (OAS; W-00-13-31465; W-00-14-31465; various reviews; expected issue date: FY 2015)

Quality of Care and Safety of Beneficiaries

> Home health services—Screenings of health care workers

We will review health-screening records of Medicaid home health agency (HHA) health care workers to determine whether they were screened in accordance with Federal and State requirements. Health screenings for home health care workers include vaccinations, such as those for hepatitis and influenza. HHAs provide health care services to Medicaid beneficiaries while the home health care workers are visiting beneficiaries' homes. HHAs must operate and provide services in compliance with all applicable Federal, State, and local laws and regulations and with accepted standards that apply to personnel providing services within such an agency. (Social Security Act, § 1891(a)(5).) The Federal requirements for home health services are found at 42 CFR §§ 440.70, 441.15, and 441.16 and at 42 CFR Part 484. Other applicable requirements are found in State and local regulations. (OAS; W-00-11-31387; various reviews; expected issue date: FY 2015)

Other Medicaid Services, Equipment, and Supplies

Acronyms and Abbreviations for Selected Terms:

CMS—Centers for Medicare & Medicaid Services
EPSDT—Early and Periodic Screening, Diagnostic, and
Treatment (services)

FMAP—Federal medical assistance percentage
LTSS—long-term services and support

Policies and Practices

➢ Medical equipment and supplies—Opportunities to reduce Medicaid payment rates for selected items

We will determine whether opportunities exist for lowering Medicaid payments for some medical equipment and supplies. We will also determine the amount of Medicaid savings that could be achieved for selected items through rebates, competitive bidding, or other means. Prior work found that State Medicaid programs negotiated rebates with manufacturers that reduced net payments for home blood glucose test strips. Similarly, CMS reduced Part B rates of payment in selected areas through competitive bidding. (OAS; W-00-13-31390; W-00-15-31390; various reviews; expected issue date: FY 2015)

Billing and Payments

➢ Transportation services—Compliance with Federal and State requirements

We will review Medicaid payments by States to providers for transportation services to determine the appropriateness of the payments for such services. Federal regulations require States to ensure necessary transportation for Medicaid beneficiaries to and from providers. (42 CFR § 431.53.) Each State may have different Medicaid coverage criteria, reimbursement rates, rules governing covered services, and beneficiary eligibility for services. (OAS; W-00-13-31121; various reviews; expected issue date: FY 2015)

➢ Health-care-acquired conditions—Prohibition on Federal reimbursements

We will determine whether selected States made Medicaid payments for hospital care associated with health-care-acquired conditions and provider-preventable conditions and quantify the amount of Medicaid payments for such conditions. As of July 1, 2011, Federal payments to States are prohibited for any amounts expended for providing medical assistance for health-care-acquired conditions. (Social Security Act, § 1903, and ACA, § 2702.) Federal regulations prohibit Medicaid payments by States for services related to health-care-acquired conditions and for provider-preventable conditions as defined by CMS or included in the Medicaid State Plan. (42 CFR § 447.26.) (OAS; W-00-14-31452; various reviews; expected issue date: FY 2015; ACA)

State Claims for Federal Reimbursement

➢ Dental services for children—Inappropriate billing

We will review Medicaid payments by States for dental services to determine whether States have properly claimed Federal reimbursement. Prior OIG work indicated that some dental providers may be inappropriately billing for services. Dental services are required for most Medicaid-eligible individuals under age 21 as a component of the Early and Periodic Screening, Diagnostic, and Treatment (EPSDT) services benefit. (Social Security Act, §§ 1905(a)(4)(B) and 1905(r).) Federal regulations define "dental services" as diagnostic, preventative, or corrective procedures provided by or under the supervision of a dentist. (42 CFR § 440.100.) Services include the treatment of teeth and the associated structure of the oral cavity and disease, injury, or impairment that may affect the oral cavity or general health of the recipient. (OAS; W-00-13-31135; various reviews; expected issue date: FY 2015)

➢ Family planning services—Claims for enhanced Federal funding

We will review family planning services in several States to determine whether States improperly claimed enhanced Federal funding for such services and the resulting financial impact on Medicaid. Previous OIG work found improper claims for enhanced funds for family planning services. States may claim Federal reimbursement for family planning services at the enhanced Federal matching rate of 90 percent. (Social Security Act, § 1903(a)(5).) (OAS; W-00-13-31078; W-00-14-31078; W-00-15-31078; various reviews; expected issue date: FY 2015)

➢ Community First Choice State plan option under the Affordable Care Act (new)

We will review Community First Choice (CFC) payments to determine whether the payments are proper and allowable. The ACA, section 2401, added section 1915(k) to the Social Security Act, a new Medicaid State plan option that allows States to provide statewide home and community-based attendant services and support to individuals who would otherwise require an institutional level of care. States taking up the option will receive a 6-percent increase in their FMAP for CFC services. To be eligible for CFC services, beneficiaries must otherwise require an institutional level of care and meet financial eligibility criteria. (OAS; W-00-15-31495; expected issue date: FY 2016; ACA)

➢ Payments to States under the Balancing Incentive Program (new)

We will review expenditures the States claimed under the Balancing Incentive Program (BIP) to ensure that they were for eligible Medicaid long-term services and support (LTSS) and determine whether the States used the additional enhanced Federal match in accordance with § 10202 of the ACA. Under the BIP, eligible States can receive either a 2-percent or 5-percent increase in their FMAP for eligible Medicaid LTSS expenditures. Funding to States under the BIP cannot exceed $3 billion over the program's 4-year period (i.e., October 1, 2011, through September 30, 2015). To receive payments, participating States agree to make structural changes to increase access to non-institutional LTSS. Additionally, the States must use the additional Federal funding to provide new or expanded offerings of non-institutional LTSS. (OAS; W-00-15-31482; various reviews; expected issue date: FY 2016; ACA)

Quality of Care and Safety of Beneficiaries

> ## Access to pediatric dental care for children enrolled in Medicaid

We will review billing patterns of pediatric dentists and their associated clinics in selected States and describe the extent to which children enrolled in Medicaid received dental services in these States. In recent years, a number of dental providers and chains have been prosecuted for providing unnecessary dental procedures and causing harm to Medicaid children. In addition, children's access to dental services has been a longstanding Medicaid problem. Medicaid covers comprehensive dental care for approximately 37 million low-income children through the EPSDT benefit. Under EPSDT, States must cover dental services and dental screening services for children. (OEI; 02-14-00480; 02-14-00490; various reviews; expected issue date: FY 2015)

> ## Utilization of preventive screening services for children enrolled in Medicaid

We will determine what steps CMS has taken to address OIG's recommendations to improve the provision of Medicaid EPSDT services. We will also determine whether the underuse of EPSDT services continues to be a challenge for children enrolled in Medicaid. Previous OIG work found that, in nine States, three out of four children did not receive all required medical, vision, and hearing screenings. OIG made several recommendations to CMS to increase participation in EPSDT screenings and to increase the completeness of medical screenings. (OEI; 05-13-00690; expected issue date: FY 2015)

> ## Medicaid beneficiary transfers from group homes and nursing facilities to hospital emergency rooms (new)

We will review the rate of and reasons for transfer from group homes or nursing facilities to hospital emergency departments. High occurrences of emergency transfers could indicate poor quality. Prior OIG work examined transfers to hospital emergency departments, raising concerns about the quality of care provided in some nursing facilities. There is congressional interest in this area. (OAS; W-00-15-31040; various reviews; expected issue date: FY 2015)

State Management of Medicaid

Acronyms and Abbreviations for Selected Terms:

CMS—Centers for Medicare & Medicaid Services	MIP—Medicaid Integrity Program
CPE—certified public expenditures	MFCU—Medicaid Fraud Control Unit
FFP—Federal financial participation	OMB—Office of Management and Budget
FMAP—Federal medical assistance percentage	RMSS—random moment sampling systems
Form CMS-64—Quarterly Medicaid Statement of Expenditures	

How States Fund Their Medicaid Programs

> ## State use of provider taxes to generate Federal funding

We will review State health-care-related taxes imposed on various Medicaid providers to determine whether the taxes comply with applicable Federal requirements. Our work will focus on the mechanism States use to raise revenue through provider taxes and determine the amount of Federal funding generated. Previous OIG work raised concerns about States' use of health-care-related taxes. Many States finance a portion of their Medicaid spending by imposing taxes on health care providers. Federal regulations define and set forth the standard for permissible health-care-related taxes. (42 CFR §§ 433.55 and 433.68.) (OAS; W-00-14-31455; various reviews; expected issue date: FY 2015)

State compliance with Federal Certified Public Expenditures regulations

We will determine whether States are complying with Federal regulations for claiming Certified Public Expenditures (CPEs), which are normally generated by local governments as part of their contribution to the coverage of Medicaid services. States may claim CPEs to provide the States' shares in claiming Federal reimbursement as long as the CPEs comply with Federal regulations and are being used for the required purposes. (42 CFR § 433.51 and 45 CFR § 95.13.) (OAS; W-00-14-31110; various reviews; expected issue date: FY 2015)

State Claims for Federal Reimbursement

State allocation of Medicaid administrative costs

We will review administrative costs claimed by several States to determine whether they were properly allocated and claimed or directly charged to Medicaid. Prior reviews in a State noted problems with the State's administrative costs. The Federal share of Medicaid administrative costs is typically 50 percent, with enhanced rates for specific types of costs. Federal cost sharing for the proper and efficient administration of Medicaid State plans is provided by the Social Security Act, § 1903(a)(7). Administrative costs are claimed in accordance with Office of Management and Budget (OMB) Circular A-87, *Cost Principles for State, Local, and Indian Tribal Governments* and State requirements. (OAS; W-00-15-31123; various reviews; expected issue date: FY 2015)

State cost allocations that deviate from acceptable practices

We will review public assistance cost allocation plans and processes for selected States to determine whether the States claimed Medicaid costs that were supported and allocated on the basis of random moment sampling systems (RMSS) that deviated from acceptable statistical sampling practices. Prior OIG reviews of school-based and community-based administrative claims found significant unallowable payments when payments were based on RMSS. Such systems must be documented so as to support the propriety of the costs assigned to Federal awards. (OMB Circular A-87, *Cost Principles for State, Local, and Indian Tribal Governments*, Attachment A, § C.1.j.) A State must claim Federal financial participation (FFP) for costs associated with a program only in accordance with its approved cost allocation plan (45 CFR § 95.517(a).) (OAS; W-00-13-31467; W-00-14-31467; various reviews; expected issue date: FY 2015)

Enhanced Federal Medical Assistance Percentage

We will review States' Medicaid claims to determine whether the States correctly applied enhanced FMAP payment provisions of the ACA. The ACA, § 2001, authorized the use of an FMAP of 100 percent for individuals who are newly eligible because of Medicaid expansion. In addition, the ACA, § 2012, required that Medicaid payments to primary care providers be at least those of the

Medicare rates in effect for calendar years 2013 and 2014. (OAS; W-00-14-31480; W-00-15-31480; various reviews; expected issue date: FY 2015; ACA)

> ## Medicaid eligibility determinations in selected States

We will determine the extent to which selected States made inaccurate Medicaid eligibility determinations. We will examine eligibility inaccuracy for Medicaid beneficiaries in selected States that expanded their Medicaid programs pursuant to the ACA and in States that did not. We will also assess whether and how the selected States addressed issues that contributed to inaccurate determinations. For some States, we will calculate a Medicaid eligibility error rate and determine the amount of payments associated with beneficiaries who received incorrect eligibility determinations. The ACA, § 2001, required significant changes affecting State processes for Medicaid enrollment, modified criteria for Medicaid eligibility, and authorized the use of an enhanced FMAP of 100 percent for newly eligible individuals. (OAS; W-00-14-31140; W-00-15-31140; various reviews; and OEI; 06-14-00330; expected issue date: FY 2015; ACA)

State Adjustments of Federal Reimbursement

> ## State Medicaid monetary drawdowns—Reconciliation with Form CMS-64

We will review the Medicaid monetary drawdowns that States received from the Federal Reserve System to determine whether they were supported by actual expenditures reported by the States on Quarterly Medicaid Statement of Expenditures (Form CMS-64). States draw monetary advances against a continuing letter of credit certified to the Secretary of the Treasury in favor of the State payee throughout a quarter. (42 CFR § 430.30(d)(4).) After the end of each quarter, States must submit Form CMS-64, which shows the disposition of Medicaid funds used to pay for actual medical and administrative expenditures for the reporting period. (42 CFR § 430.30(c).) The amounts reported on Form CMS-64 should reconcile the monetary advances for a quarter. (OAS; W-00-13-31456; various reviews; expected issue date: FY 2015)

> ## State reporting of Medicaid collections on Form CMS-64

We will determine whether States accurately captured Medicaid collections on Form CMS-64 and returned the correct Federal share related to those collections. Previous OIG work revealed multiple errors in compiling collection amounts on Form CMS-64, particularly errors related to the calculation of the Federal share returned. Collections decrease the total expenditures reported for the period. (42 CFR §§ 433.154 and 433.320.) States should compute the Federal share of collections at the rate at which the Federal Government matched the original expenditures. (CMS's *State Medicaid Manual*, § 2500.1(B).) (OAS; W-00-14-31457; various reviews; expected issue date: FY 2015)

> ## State use of incorrect FMAP for Federal share adjustments

We will review States' Medicaid claims records to determine whether the States used the correct FMAP when processing claim adjustments reported on Form CMS-64. We reviewed the claim adjustments reported on Form CMS-64 for one State and determined that it did not use the correct FMAP for the majority of adjustments. The Federal Government is required to reimburse a State at the FMAP rate in effect at the time the expenditure was made. (Social Security Act, § 1903(a)(1).) (OAS; W-00-14-31460; various reviews; expected issue date: FY 2015)

State Program Integrity Activities and Compliance With Federal Requirements

> ## State actions to address vulnerabilities identified during CMS reviews

We will review corrective actions that State Medicaid agencies have implemented to address the findings and recommendations from State Medicaid program integrity reviews conducted by CMS. We will determine why States have not implemented all corrective actions, examine the followup CMS performed to ensure that corrective actions were taken by States, and examine the evidence CMS reviews to ensure that corrective actions were implemented. As part of its Medicaid Integrity Program (MIP) activities, CMS conducts a triennial review of each State's program integrity functions to assess their effectiveness and compliance with Federal requirements. CMS issues to the State a final report of findings and recommendations and requires the State to provide a corrective action plan within 30 days of the report issuance. The MIP was established by the DRA, § 6034. (OEI; 00-00-00000; expected issue date: FY 2016)

> ## State terminations of providers terminated by Medicare or by other States

We will review States' compliance with a new requirement that they terminate their Medicaid program providers that have been terminated under Medicare or by another State Medicaid program. We will determine whether such providers are terminated by all State Medicaid programs in which they are enrolled, assess the status of the supporting information-sharing system, determine how CMS is ensuring that States share complete and accurate information, and identify obstacles States face in complying with the termination requirement. The new requirement became effective January 1, 2011. (Social Security Act, § 1902(a)(39), as amended by the ACA, § 6501.) (OEI; 06-12-00030; expected issue date: FY 2015; ACA)

> ## Recovering Medicaid overpayments—Credit balances in Medicaid patient accounts

We will review providers' patient accounts to determine whether there are Medicaid overpayments in accounts with credit balances. Previous OIG work found Medicaid overpayments in patients' accounts with credit balances. Credit balances generally occur when the reimbursement that a provider receives for services provided to a Medicaid beneficiary exceeds the charges billed, such as when a provider receives a duplicate payment for the same service from the Medicaid program or another third party payer. In such cases, the provider should return the overpayment to the Medicaid program. When there is more than one payer, Medicaid is the payer of last resort. (Social Security Act, § 1902(a)(25); 42 CFR Part 433, Subpart D; various State laws; and CMS's *State Medicaid Manual*, Pub. No. 45, Part 3, § 3900.1.) (OAS; W-00-13-31311; various reviews; expected issue date: FY 2015)

> ## State and CMS collection and verification of provider ownership information

We will determine the extent to which States and CMS collect and verify required ownership information for provider entities enrolled in Medicare and Medicaid. We will also review States' and CMS's practices for collecting and verifying provider ownership information and determine whether States and CMS had comparable provider ownership information for providers enrolled in Medicaid and/or Medicare. Federal regulations require Medicaid and Medicare providers to disclose ownership information, such as the name, address, and date of birth of each person with an ownership or controlling interest in the provider entity. (42 CFR § 455.104.) (OEI; 04-11-00590, 04-11-00591, 04-11-00592; expected issue date: FY 2015)

> ## States' experiences with enhanced provider screening

We will review States' use of enhanced screenings that assess risk for fraud, waste, and abuse for moderate- and high-risk enrolling and revalidating Medicaid providers and suppliers. We will also determine the results of States' efforts to prevent risky providers and suppliers from participating in Medicaid before and after the implementation of enhanced screenings. The ACA, § 6402, requires enhanced screening for providers and suppliers seeking initial enrollment, re-enrollment, or revalidation in Medicare, Medicaid, and the Children's Health Insurance Program (CHIP). States are responsible for employing screening and revalidation procedures for their Medicaid and CHIP providers. (OEI; 05-13-00520; expected issue date: FY 2015; ACA)

> ## Provider payment suspensions during pending investigations of credible fraud allegations

We will review payments to providers with allegations of fraud deemed credible by States. We will also review States' processes for suspending payments. FFP in Medicaid is not available for items or services furnished by an individual or entity when the State has failed to suspend payments during a period when there is a credible allegation of fraud. (Social Security Act, § 1903(i)(2), as amended by the ACA, § 6402(h)(2).) Upon determinations that allegations of fraud are credible, States must suspend all Medicaid payments to the providers, unless the States have good cause to not suspend payments or to suspend payment only in part. (42 CFR § 455.23(a).) States are required to make fraud referrals to Medicaid Fraud Control Units (MFCUs) or to appropriate law enforcement agencies in States with no certified MFCUs. (42 CFR § 455.23(d).) We will determine whether select Medicaid State agencies are in compliance with these provisions. (OAS; W-00-14-31473; various reviews; expected issue date: FY 2015; and OEI; 09-14-00020; expected issue date: FY 2015; ACA)

OIG Oversight of State Medicaid Fraud Control Units

> ## Reviews of State Medicaid Fraud Control Units

We will continue to conduct indepth onsite reviews of the management, operations, and performance of a sample of MFCUs. We will identify effective practices and areas for improvement in MFCU management and operations. As part of its responsibility for administering Federal grants to MFCUs, OIG provides oversight and guidance to MFCUs, assesses MFCU compliance with Federal regulations and policy, and evaluates MFCU performance under established performance standards. The onsite reviews are part of OIG's program of oversight for MFCUs that includes annual recertification, training, and collection and reporting of statistical information. (OEI; 00-00-00000; various reviews; expected issue date: FY 2015)

> ## States and territories without Medicaid Fraud Control Units

We will determine whether each of the U.S. territories, none of which currently operates a MFCU, has sought an exemption as part of its State Medicaid plan, as required by section 1902(a)(61) of the Social Security Act. We will also determine whether North Dakota, the only State that does not have a MFCU and that received an exemption in 1994, continues to operate under the conditions that supported the State's exemption. Each State and territory must maintain a certified MFCU as part of a State Medicaid program, unless the Secretary determines that operation of a MFCU would not be cost effective and that other safeguards are in place. (Social Security Act, §§ 1902(a)(61) and 1101(a)(1).) The District of Columbia and 49 States have established MFCUs. The territories of American Samoa, Guam, the Northern Mariana Islands, Puerto Rico, and the U.S. Virgin Islands also have not established MFCUs but are required to operate MFCUs as part of their Medicaid programs or receive an exemption. (OEI; 00-00-00000; expected issue date: FY 2016)

Medicaid Information System Controls and Security

Acronyms and Abbreviations for Selected Terms:

MCO—managed care organization
MSIS—Medicaid Statistical Information System

NCCI—National Correct Coding initiative

Controls To Prevent Improper Medicaid Payments

➤ Duplicate payments for beneficiaries with multiple Medicaid identification numbers

We will review duplicate payments made by States on behalf of Medicaid beneficiaries with multiple Medicaid identification numbers and identify States' procedures or other controls for preventing such payments. A preliminary data match identified a significant number of individuals who were assigned more than one Medicaid identification number and for whom multiple Medicaid payments were made for the same period. (OAS; W-00-14-31374; various reviews; expected issue date: FY 2015)

➤ National Correct Coding Initiative edits and CMS oversight

We will review selected States' implementation of National Correct Coding initiative (NCCI) edits for Medicaid claims and describe CMS's oversight of NCCI edits. The NCCI consists of coding policies and automatic computer edits. The NCCI's original purpose was to promote correct coding of health care services provided to Medicare beneficiaries and to prevent payment for improperly coded services. Federal law required States to incorporate methodologies compatible with NCCI for Medicaid claims filed on or after October 1, 2010. (Social Security Act, § 1903(r), as amended by the ACA, § 6507.) States were permitted to deactivate some or all NCCI edits because of conflicts with State laws, regulations, administrative rules, payment policies, and/or the States' levels of operational readiness. (State Medicaid Director Letter #10-017.) As of April 1, 2011, lack of operational readiness was no longer a permissible basis for deactivation of the edits. (State Medicaid Director Letter #11-003.) After April 1, 2011, the only basis for deactivation is conflicts with State laws, regulations, administrative rules, and/or payments policies. (OAS; W-00-15-31459; various reviews; expected issue date: FY 2015; and OEI; 09-14-00440; expected issue date: FY 2015, ACA)

Controls To Ensure the Security of Medicaid Systems and Information

> ## CMS oversight of States' Medicaid information systems security controls

We will determine the adequacy of CMS's oversight of States' Medicaid system and information security controls, including the policies, technical assistance, and security and operational guidance provided to the States. For selected States, we will use OIG's automated assessment tools to assess controls for their information system networks, databases, Web-facing applications, logical access, and wireless access. We will also review general controls, such as disaster recovery plans and physical security. Prior OIG audits reported that States lack sufficient security features, potentially exposing Medicaid beneficiary health information to unauthorized access. State system controls for Medicaid data and transactions have not been consistently applied and have not been adequately monitored by CMS pursuant to Federal requirements for Automated Data Processing System Security and Review (45 CFR § 95.621(f).) CMS is responsible for ensuring that appropriate security controls have been implemented. (OAS; W-00-14-40019; W-00-15-40019; various reviews; expected issue date: FY 2015)

Medicaid Managed Care

Managed care is a health delivery system that aims to maximize efficiency by negotiating rates, coordinating care, and managing the use of services. State Medicaid agencies contract with MCOs to provide comprehensive health services in return for a fixed, prospective payment (capitated payment) for each enrolled beneficiary.

Acronyms and Abbreviations for Selected Terms:

GAO— Government Accountability Office   MSIS—Medicaid Statistical Information System
MCO—managed care organization   OMB—Office of Management and Budget

State Payments to Managed Care Entities

> ## Medicaid managed care reimbursement

We will review States' managed care plan reimbursements to determine whether MCOs are appropriately and correctly reimbursed for services provided. We will ensure that the data used to set rates are reliable and include only costs for services covered under the State plan as required by or costs of services authorized by CMS. (42 CFR §438.6(e).) Also, we will verify that payments made under a risk-sharing mechanism and incentive payments made to MCOs are within the limits set forth in Federal regulations. (42 CFR § 438.6(c)(5)(ii) and 42 CFR § 438.6(c)(5)(iii) and (iv).) Previous work by the Government Accountability Office (GAO) found that CMS's oversight of States' rate-setting required improvement and that States may not audit or independently verify the MCO-reported data used to set rates. (GAO-10-810.) (OAS; W-00-14-31471; various reviews; expected issue date: FY 2015)

Medical loss ratio—Managed care plans' refunds to States

We will review managed care plans with contract provisions that require a minimum percentage of total costs to be expended for medical services (medical loss ratio) to determine whether a refund was made to the State agency when the minimum medical loss ratio threshold was not met. We will also determine whether plan expenses were properly classified as medical or administrative. Prior OIG work found that although the minimum medical loss ratios were not met, the managed care plans did not make the required refunds to the State. States must properly report expenditures and apply any applicable credits (such as refunds). (OMB Circular A-87, *Cost Principles for State, Local, and Indian Tribal Governments*.) (OAS; W-00-13-31372; various reviews; expected issue date: FY 2015)

MCO payments for services after beneficiaries' deaths (new)

We will identify Medicaid managed care payments made on behalf of deceased beneficiaries. We will also identify trends in Medicaid claims with service dates after beneficiaries' dates of death. Prior OIG reports have found that Medicare paid for services that purportedly started or continued after beneficiaries' dates of death. (OAS; W-00-15-31497; expected issue date: FY 2016)

MCO payments for ineligible beneficiaries (new)

We will identify Medicaid managed care payments made on behalf of beneficiaries that were not eligible for Medicaid. We will also identify trends in Medicaid claims within this population. Section 1903(m) of the Social Security Act authorizes payments to States for eligible Medicaid beneficiaries enrolled in an MCO. Prior OIG work has found that Medicaid paid for services that purportedly started or continued during periods where the beneficiary was not eligible for Medicaid. (OAS; W-00-15-31498; expected issue date: FY 2016)

Data Collection and Reporting

Completeness and accuracy of managed care encounter data

We will determine the extent to which complete Medicaid managed care encounter data are included in Medicaid Statistical Management System (MSIS). We will also identify factors that enable States and Medicaid managed care entities to collect and report MSIS encounter data or prevent them from performing these functions. Finally, we will assess CMS's oversight of the reporting of MSIS encounter data. A prior OIG review of 2007 data found that although all 40 States with Medicaid managed care were collecting encounter data and most of those States used the data, only 25 States included the data in their MSIS submissions to CMS. Of the 25 States that included encounter data in their MSIS submissions, the MSIS files containing encounter data varied by service (e.g., inpatient, pharmacy, long-term care) and eligibility, as did the data elements reported in each file. Federal law requires States and MCOs to submit data elements deemed necessary by the Secretary for use in program integrity, program oversight, and administration. (ACA, § 6504.) Federal Medicaid matching funds for the operation of an MSIS are authorized pursuant to the Social Security Act, § 1903(a)(3)(B). Such matching funds can be withheld from States that fail to submit required Medicaid data, including encounter data. (Social Security Act, §§ 1903(m)(2)(A) and 1903(r)(1).) (OEI; 07-13-00120; expected issue date: FY 2015; ACA)

Program Integrity in Managed Care

> ## Medicaid managed care entities' identification of fraud and abuse

We will determine whether Medicaid MCOs identified and addressed potential fraud and abuse incidents. We will also describe how States oversee MCOs' efforts to identify and address fraud and abuse. A prior OIG report revealed that over a quarter of the MCOs surveyed did not report a single case of suspected fraud and abuse to their State Medicaid agencies in 2009. The report also found that MCOs and States are taking steps to address fraud and abuse in managed care and they remain concerned about their prevalence. All MCOs are required to have processes to detect, correct, and prevent fraud, waste, and abuse. However, the Federal requirements surrounding these activities are general in nature (42 CFR § 438.608), and MCOs vary widely in how they deter fraud, waste, and abuse. (OEI; 02-13-00640; expected issue date: FY 2016)

Beneficiary Protections in Managed Care

> ## Beneficiary access to services under Medicaid managed care

We will review Medicaid managed care provider networks and describe the extent to which managed care beneficiaries have access to services. We will also describe State standards for ensuring access to primary and specialty care and will determine the extent to which States identify and address problems with access to care in their managed care plans. States must ensure that managed care plans maintain and monitor a network of providers that is sufficient to provide adequate access to all Medicaid services. (42 CFR §§ 438.202-210.) In establishing and maintaining this network, managed care plans must consider the anticipated Medicaid enrollment, the expected use of services, the number and types of providers accepting new patients, and the locations of providers and beneficiaries. (OEI; 02-13-00670; expected issue date: FY 2015)

> ## Medicaid managed care beneficiary grievances and appeals process

We will review the extent to which States monitor Medicaid MCOs' grievances and appeals systems for compliance with Federal requirements. States are required to provide an opportunity for a fair hearing to any beneficiary whose Medicaid claim for assistance is denied or not acted upon promptly. (Social Security Act, § 1902(a)(3).) Medicaid managed care entities are required to establish internal grievance procedures under which beneficiaries, or providers acting on their behalf, may challenge the denial of coverage of, or payment for, medical services. (Social Security Act, § 1932(b)(4).) (OEI; 00-00-00000; expected issue date: FY 2016)

> ## Oversight of managed care entities' marketing practices

We will review State Medicaid agencies' oversight policies, procedures, and activities to determine the extent to which States monitor Medicaid MCOs' marketing practices and compliance with Federal and State contractual marketing requirements. We will also determine the extent to which CMS ensures that States comply with Federal requirements involving Medicaid MCO marketing practices. No marketing materials may be distributed by Medicaid MCOs without first obtaining States' approval. (Social Security Act, § 1932(d)(2).) States are permitted to impose additional requirements in contracts with MCOs about marketing activities. (42 CFR § 438.104.) (OEI; 00-00-00000; expected issue date: FY 2016)

Acronyms and Abbreviations for Selected Terms:

CIA—corporate integrity agreement
CMP—civil monetary penalty
CMS—Centers for Medicare & Medicaid Services
CPG—compliance program guidance

DOJ—Department of Justice
HEAT—Health Care Fraud Prevention and Enforcement
Action Team
MFCU—[State] Medicaid Fraud Control Unit

Legal Activities

The Office of Inspector General's (OIG) resolution of civil and administrative health care fraud cases includes litigation of program exclusions and civil monetary penalties (CMPs) and assessments. OIG also negotiates and monitors corporate integrity agreements (CIAs) and issues fraud alerts, advisory bulletins, and advisory opinions. OIG develops regulations within its scope of authority, including safe harbor regulations under the anti-kickback statute, and provides compliance program guidance (CPG). OIG encourages health care providers to promptly self-disclose conduct that violates Federal health care program requirements and provides them a self-disclosure protocol and guidance.

Exclusions From Program Participation

OIG may exclude individuals and entities from participation in Medicare, Medicaid, and all other Federal health care programs for many reasons, some of which include program-related convictions, patient abuse or neglect convictions, licensing board disciplinary actions, or other actions that pose a risk to beneficiaries or programs. (Social Security Act, § 1128, § 1156, and other statutes.) Exclusions are generally based on referrals from Federal and State agencies. We work with these agencies to ensure the timely referral of convictions and licensing board and administrative actions. In fiscal year (FY) 2014, OIG excluded 4,017 individuals and entities from participation in Federal health care programs. Searchable exclusion lists are available on OIG's Web site at:

- http://exclusions.oig.hhs.gov/

Civil Monetary Penalties

OIG pursues CMP cases, when supported by appropriate evidence, on the basis of the submission of false or fraudulent claims; the offer, payment, solicitation, or receipt of remuneration (kickbacks) in violation of the Social Security Act, § 1128B(b); violations of the Emergency Medical Treatment and Labor Act of 1986; items and services furnished to patients of a quality that fails to meet professionally recognized standards of health care; and other conduct actionable under the Social Security Act, § 1128A, or other CMP authorities delegated to OIG.

False Claims Act Cases and Corporate Integrity Agreements

When adequate evidence of violations exists, OIG staff members work closely with prosecutors from the Department of Justice (DOJ) to develop and pursue Federal false claims cases against individuals and entities that defraud the Government. Authorities relevant to this work come from the False Claims Amendments Act of 1986 and the Fraud Enforcement and Recovery Act of 2009. We assist DOJ prosecutors in litigation and settlement negotiations arising from these cases. We also consider whether to invoke our exclusion authority on the basis of the defendants' conduct. When appropriate and necessary, we require defendants to implement CIAs aimed at ensuring compliance with Federal health care program requirements.

Providers' Compliance With Corporate Integrity Agreements

OIG often negotiates compliance obligations with health care providers and other entities as part of the settlement of Federal health care program investigations arising under a variety of civil false claims statutes. Subsequently, OIG assesses providers' compliance with the terms of the CIAs. For example, we conduct site visits to entities that are subject to CIAs to verify compliance, to confirm information submitted to us by the entities, and to assess the providers' compliance programs. We review a variety of information submitted by providers to determine whether their compliance mechanisms are appropriate and identify problems and establish a basis for corrective action. When warranted, we impose sanctions, in the form of stipulated penalties or exclusions, on providers that breach CIA obligations. Current CIAs and other integrity agreements are listed on OIG's Web site at:

- http://oig.hhs.gov/fraud/cia/cia_list.asp

Advisory Opinions and Other Industry Guidance

To foster compliance by providers and industry groups, OIG responds to requests for formal advisory opinions on applying the anti-kickback statute and other fraud and abuse statutes to specific business arrangements or practices. Advisory opinions provide meaningful advice on statutes in specific factual situations. We also issue special fraud alerts and advisory bulletins about practices that we determine are suspect and CPG for specific areas. Examples are available on OIG's Web site at:

- Advisory Opinions: http://oig.hhs.gov/fraud/advisoryopinions.asp
- Fraud Alerts: http://oig.hhs.gov/compliance/alerts/index.asp
- Compliance Guidance: http://oig.hhs.gov/fraud/complianceguidance.asp
- Open Letters: http://oig.hhs.gov/fraud/openletters.asp
- Other Guidance: http://oig.hhs.gov/compliance/alerts/guidance/index.asp

Provider Self-Disclosure

OIG is committed to assisting health care providers and suppliers in detecting and preventing fraud and abuse. Since 1998, we have made available comprehensive guidelines describing the process for providers to voluntarily submit self-disclosures to OIG of fraud, waste, or abuse. The Provider Self-Disclosure Protocol gives providers an opportunity to minimize the potential costs and disruption that a full-scale OIG audit or investigation might entail if fraud is uncovered. The self-disclosure also enables the provider to negotiate a fair monetary settlement and potentially avoid being excluded from participation in Federal health care programs.

The protocol guides providers and suppliers through the process of structuring a disclosure to OIG about matters that constitute potential violations of Federal laws (as opposed to honest mistakes that may have resulted in being overpaid by a Federal program). The provider or supplier is expected to thoroughly investigate the nature and cause of the matters uncovered and make a reliable assessment of their economic impact (e.g., an estimate of the losses to Federal health care programs). OIG evaluates the reported results of each internal investigation to determine the appropriate course of action. The self-disclosure guidelines are available on the OIG Web site at:

- http://oig.hhs.gov/fraud/selfdisclosure.asp.

On April 17, 2013, OIG updated its Provider Self-Disclosure Protocol, which is available at:

- http://oig.hhs.gov/compliance/self-disclosure-info/files/Provider-Self-Disclosure-Protocol.pdf

Investigative Activities

OIG conducts and coordinates criminal, civil, and administrative investigations of fraud, waste, abuse, and misconduct related to more than 100 Department of Health and Human Services (HHS) programs and operations. The investigations include Medicare and Medicaid fraud, failure-of-care cases, child support enforcement violations, grant and contract fraud, network intrusions, and employee misconduct. Investigations can lead to criminal prosecutions and program exclusions; recovery of damages and penalties through criminal, civil, and administrative proceedings; and corrective management actions, regulations, or legislation. Each year, thousands of complaints from various sources are brought to OIG's attention for review, investigation, and resolution. The nature and volume of complaints and priority of issues vary from year to year. We describe some of the more significant investigative outcomes in OIG's *Semiannual Report(s) to Congress*, which are available on our Web site at:

- http://oig.hhs.gov/publications.asp.

See OIG's Consumer Alerts at:

- http://oig.hhs.gov/fraud/consumer-alerts/index.asp.

Medicare Fraud Strike Force Teams and Other Collaboration

OIG devotes significant resources to investigating Medicare and Medicaid fraud. We conduct investigations in conjunction with other law enforcement entities, such as the Federal Bureau of Investigation, the U.S. Postal Inspection Service, the Internal Revenue Service, and State Medicaid Fraud Control Units (MFCUs).

The Health Care Fraud Prevention and Enforcement Action Team (HEAT) was started in 2009 by HHS and DOJ to strengthen programs and invest in new resources and technologies to prevent and combat health care fraud, waste, and abuse. Using a collaborative model, Medicare Fraud Strike Force teams coordinate law enforcement operations among Federal, State, and local law enforcement entities. These teams, now a key component of HEAT, have a record of successfully analyzing data to quickly identify and prosecute fraud.

Strike Force teams were formed in March 2007 and are operating in nine major cities. The effectiveness of the Strike Force model is enhanced by interagency collaboration within HHS. For example, we refer credible allegations of fraud to the Centers for Medicare & Medicaid Services (CMS) so it can suspend payments as appropriate. During Strike Force operations, OIG and CMS work to impose payment suspensions that immediately prevent losses from claims submitted by Strike Force targets. In support of Strike Force operations, OIG:

- investigates individuals, facilities, or entities that, for example, bill or are alleged to have billed Medicare and/or Medicaid for services not rendered, claims that manipulate payment codes to inflate reimbursement amounts, and false claims submitted to obtain program funds;

- investigates business arrangements that allegedly violate the Federal health care anti-kickback statute and the statutory limitation on self-referrals by physicians; and

- examines quality-of-care and failure-of-care issues in nursing facilities, institutions, community-based settings, and other care settings and instances in which Federal programs may have been billed for services that were medically unnecessary, were not rendered, or were not rendered as prescribed or in which the care was so deficient that it constituted "worthless services."

Other areas of investigation include Medicare and Medicaid drug benefit issues and assisting CMS in identifying program vulnerabilities and schemes, such as prescription shorting (a pharmacy's dispensing of fewer doses of a drug than prescribed, but charging the full amount).

Working with law enforcement partners at the Federal, State, and local levels, we investigate schemes that illegally market, obtain, and distribute prescription drugs. In doing so, we seek to protect Medicare and Medicaid from making improper payments, deter the illegal use of prescription drugs, and curb the danger associated with street distribution of highly addictive medications.

We assist MFCUs in investigating allegations of false claims submitted to Medicaid and will continue to strengthen coordination between OIG and organizations such as the National Association of Medicaid Fraud Control Units and the National Association for Medicaid Program Integrity. Highlights of recent enforcement actions to which OIG has contributed are posted to OIG's Web site at http://oig.hhs.gov/fraud/enforcement/criminal/.

Public Health Reviews

Public health activities and programs represent the country's primary defense against acute and chronic diseases and disabilities and provide the foundation for the Nation's efforts to promote and enhance the health of the American people. Our reviews of public health agencies within the Department of Health and Human Services (HHS) generally include the following:

- **Agency for Healthcare Research and Quality (AHRQ).** AHRQ sponsors and conducts research that provides evidence-based information on health care outcomes, quality, costs, use, and access.
- **Centers for Disease Control and Prevention (CDC).** CDC operates a health surveillance system to monitor and prevent disease outbreaks, including bioterrorism; implements disease prevention strategies; and maintains national health statistics.
- **Food and Drug Administration (FDA).** FDA is responsible for ensuring the safety of the Nation's food, drugs, medical devices, biologics, cosmetics, and animal food and drugs.
- **Health Resources and Services Administration (HRSA).** HRSA maintains a safety net of health services for people who have low incomes or are uninsured or who live in rural areas or urban neighborhoods where health care is scarce.
- **Indian Health Service (IHS).** IHS provides or funds health care services for American Indians and Alaska Natives.
- **National Institutes of Health (NIH).** NIH supports medical and scientific research examining the causes of and treatments for diseases, such as cancer, human immunodeficiency virus (HIV), and acquired immunodeficiency syndrome (AIDS).
- **Substance Abuse and Mental Health Services Administration (SAMHSA).** SAMHSA funds services to improve the lives of people who have or are at risk for mental and substance abuse disorders.

Issues related to public health are also addressed within the Office of the Secretary. For example, the Office of the Assistant Secretary for Preparedness and Response serves as the Secretary's principal advisor on matters related to Federal public health preparedness and response to public health emergencies. The functions of the Office of the Assistant Secretary for Health include overseeing the protection of volunteers involved in research.

Effective management of public health programs is essential to ensure that they achieve their goals and best serve the programs' intended beneficiaries. In its work planning activities in fiscal year (FY) 2015 and beyond, OIG will consider key risk areas, such as the adequacy of CDC and its public health partners' preparedness to respond to public health emergencies, including disease outbreaks. Future work planning efforts will also include examinations of access to quality services and health and safety protections, including the integrity of the food, drug, and medical supply chain.

Acronyms and Abbreviations for Selected Terms:

AHRQ—Agency for Healthcare Research and Quality
AIDS—acquired immunodeficiency syndrome
CDC—Centers for Disease Control and Prevention
CoP—conditions of participation
DHS—Department of Homeland Security
FDA—Food and Drug Administration
FDAA—Food and Drug Amendments Act of 2007
HCP— Health Center Program
HIPAA—Health Insurance Portability and Accountability Act
HRSA—Health Resources and Services Administration
IC— institute/center (NIH)
IHS—Indian Health Service
MCO— managed care organization

MRC— Medical Reserve Corps
OMB—Office of Management and Budget
NIH—National Institutes of Health
NOM— national outcome measure
PMR— postmarketing requirement
PPHF—Prevention and Public Health Fund
PSO—Patient Safety Organization
SAMHSA—Substance Abuse and Mental Health Services Administration
SAPTBG—Substance Abuse Prevention and Treatment Block Grant
SSBG—Social Services Block Grant
WTCHP—World Trade Center Health Program

Agency for Healthcare Research and Quality

➤ AHRQ—Early implementation of patient safety organizations

We will review the policies and activities of Patient Safety Organizations (PSOs) to determine the extent of hospitals' participation in such activities, identify PSOs' practices for receiving and analyzing adverse event reports, and determine the extent to which PSOs provide information to health care providers and the Network of Patient Safety Databases maintained by AHRQ. We will evaluate PSOs' efforts to identify and resolve patient safety problems in hospitals and identify any barriers to the full and effective implementation of the PSO program. A prior OIG review found that hospitals did not identify all serious adverse events, suggesting that hospital incident-reporting systems may be an unreliable source of information for PSOs. PSOs are nongovernmental entities certified by HHS to collect and analyze reports of adverse events from hospitals and other health care settings. (Patient Safety and Quality Improvement Act of 2005.) Adverse events are harm, such as infections or injury, caused to patients during medical care. (OEI; 06-14-00080; expected issue date: FY 2015)

Centers for Disease Control and Prevention

➤ CDC—World Trade Center Health Program: Review of medical claims

We will review World Trade Center Health Program (WTCHP) expenditures to assess whether internal controls have been established in the WTCHP in accordance with Office of Management and Budget (OMB) Circular A-123, *Management's Responsibility for Internal Control*. As part of our review, we will determine whether the internal controls are adequate to (1) detect and prevent fraudulent or duplicate billing and payment for inappropriate medical services and (2) prevent excessive administrative payments in accordance with OMB Circular A-122, *Cost Principle for Non-Profit Organizations*. Prior Federal audits found that CDC did not reliably estimate costs for monitoring and treating program beneficiaries. Pursuant to the legislative requirements, medical services are provided to eligible responders and survivors with health conditions related to the September 11, 2001, terrorist attacks on the World Trade Center through contracted facilities known as Clinical Centers of Excellence. The WTCHP was established in January 2011 and is administered by CDC. (James Zadroga 9/11 Health and Compensation Act of 2010 and Public Health Service Act, § 3301(d).) (OAS; W-00-14-59040; expected issue date: FY 2015)

➤ CDC—Award process for the President's Emergency Plan for AIDS Relief cooperative agreements

We will review CDC's award process for the cooperative agreements it has under the President's Emergency Plan for AIDS Relief (PEPFAR) program to ensure compliance with applicable laws, regulations, and departmental guidance. The review will include awards made to foreign and domestic recipients. During previous reviews of CDC's award monitoring process, we noted possible deficiencies, such as conflicting, missing, or inaccurate information in the Funding Opportunity Announcement and the Notice of Award. The *Grants Policy Directive*, Part 2, § 04, specifies the process for competitive review, ranking applications, approval of applications, and award policy. (OAS; W-00-13-58311; expected issue date: FY 2015)

➤ Prevention and Public Health Fund grants—CDC Oversight

We will assess the effectiveness of CDC's management of the Prevention and Public Health Fund (PPHF) program. We will also determine selected grantees' compliance with grant requirements. Section 4002 of the Patient Protection and Affordable Care Act (ACA) established the PPHF program to provide expanded and sustained national investments in prevention and public health, to improve health outcomes, and to enhance health care quality. CDC received appropriations totaling $2.2 billion during FYs 2010–2013, representing 66 percent of total PPHF dollars. Recent legislation may change CDC's PPHF allotment. (OAS; W-00-14-59027; expected issue date: FY 2015; ACA)

➤ CDC—Accountability for property

We will determine whether CDC implemented recommendations that OIG previously made on the basis of an audit of CDC's property system. CDC maintains various types of accountable property in the United States and overseas. In a previous report, we recommended that CDC improve its controls over property. Specifically, we recommended that CDC adjust the property system to reflect the results of the annual physical inventory; remove from the property system any lost or missing property; ensure that all newly acquired property items are barcoded and correctly added to the property system; and reconcile the general ledger to the property system to identify and resolve discrepancies. As of January 2013, CDC had 60,820 items of accountable property in its inventory, representing an original purchase cost of about $455 million. (OAS; W 00-14-59025; expected issue date: FY 2015)

➤ CDC—Oversight of security of the strategic national stockpiles of pharmaceuticals

We will review CDC's efforts to ensure that pharmaceutical stockpiles are secure from theft, tampering, or other loss. We will use guidelines established in the Department of Homeland Security's (DHS) *Physical Security Manual* to assess security risks at selected stockpiles. The Strategic National Stockpile program, for which CDC and DHS share management responsibility, is designed to supplement and restock State and local public health agency pharmaceutical supplies in the event of a biological or chemical incident in the United States or its territories. The stockpiles are stored at strategic locations for the most rapid distribution possible. CDC is responsible for ensuring that the materials in these facilities are adequately protected and stored. (OAS; W-00-13-58310; expected issue date: FY 2015)

Food and Drug Administration

> ## FDA—Inspection of generic drug manufacturers

We will determine the extent to which FDA conducts inspections of generic drug manufacturers. We will also describe the results of such inspections and the enforcement actions taken by FDA in response to shortcomings or deficiencies. FDA typically inspects drug manufacturing facilities before generic drug approval and conducts routine inspections of foreign and domestic manufacturers to monitor compliance with good manufacturing practices. Generic drugs are copies of FDA-approved brand-name drugs that must be equivalent to the original drugs with respect to conditions of use, active ingredient(s), route of administration, dosage form, strength, labeling, and performance characteristics. Pharmaceutical companies must receive FDA approval before marketing and manufacturing a new generic drug. (OEI; 01-13-00600; expected issue date: FY 2015)

> ## FDA—Oversight of postmarketing studies of approved drugs

We will determine the extent to which FDA requires postmarketing studies and clinical trials (referred to as postmarketing requirements, or PMRs) for new drug applications. We will also assess how FDA monitors PMRs and takes enforcement action against applicants that do not comply with them. Section 505(o)(3) of the Food and Drug Administration Amendments Act of 2007 (FDAAA) provides FDA new authority to require additional testing of an approved prescription drug or biological product to assess serious risk related to its use. Under this authority, FDA may require an applicant to conduct PMRs at the time of approval or after approval if FDA becomes aware of new safety information or an unexpected serious risk associated with the use of the drug. (OEI; 01-13-00390; expected issue date: FY 2015)

> ## FDA—FDA inspections of high-risk food facilities

We will assess FDA's designation and inspection of high-risk food facilities. FDA is responsible for safeguarding the Nation's food supply by ensuring that all food ingredients are safe and that food is free of disease-causing organisms, chemicals, or other harmful substances. To carry out this responsibility, FDA inspects food facilities to ensure food safety and compliance with regulations. The Food Safety Modernization Act mandated that FDA increase the frequency of its inspections of domestic food facilities and inspect facilities on the basis of risk; it also indicated the criteria for designating a facility as high risk. (OEI; 02-14-00420; expected issue date: FY 2015)

> ## FDA—Review of information exchange in the drug supply chain

We will review drug supply chain trading partners' (e.g., drug manufacturers, wholesale distributors, dispensers) early experiences in exchanging transaction information and transaction history as required by section 202 of the Drug Supply Chain Security Act. Transaction information includes basic information about the drug (e.g., the strength and dosage form of the product, the National

Drug Code, etc.), and the transaction history includes transaction information for every prior transaction for that drug back to the manufacturer. Together, this information forms the foundation of drug traceability and the security of the drug supply chain. Except for dispensers, trading partners must comply with the new exchange requirements by January 1, 2015, (dispensers have until July 1, 2015, to comply). We will interview trading partners about how they have successfully exchanged this information and what, if any, obstacles they have faced. (OEI; 05-14-00640; expected issue date: FY 2015)

> ## FDA—Drug sponsors' compliance with clinical trial reporting requirements

In 2007, Congress passed the FDAAA (42 U.S.C. § 282(j)) which mandated that certain clinical trials be registered and their results be reported in the clinical trial registry and reporting data bank known as ClinicalTrials.gov. These reporting requirements are an important tool that enhances FDA's ability to assess and monitor a drug's safety and efficacy. We will determine the extent to which clinical trials comply with the reporting requirements set forth by the FDAAA and the way in which FDA is ensuring that these requirements are met. (OEI; 02-14-00610; expected issue date: FY 2015)

Health Resources and Services Administration

> ## HRSA-Community health centers' compliance with grant requirements of the Affordable Care Act (new)

We will determine whether community health centers that received funds pursuant to the ACA, § 10503, are complying with Federal laws and regulations. The review will include determining the allowability of expenditures and the adequacy of accounting systems that assess and account for program income. The review is based in part on requirements of the Public Health Service Act, § 330, and Federal regulations. (OAS; W-00-14-5928; various reviews; expected issue dates: FY 2015; ACA)

> ## HRSA—Duplicate discounts for 340B purchased drugs (new)

We will assess the risk of duplicate discounts for 340B-purchased drugs paid through Medicaid managed care organizations (MCOs) and describe States' efforts to prevent them. The ACA § 2501 required States to begin collecting rebates for drugs paid through Medicaid MCOs and prohibited duplicate discounts under the 340B Program for such drugs. However, existing tools and processes used to prevent duplicate discounts in fee-for-service Medicaid may not be sufficient for drugs paid through Medicaid MCOs. (OEI; 05-14-00430; expected issue date: FY 2015; ACA)

> ## HRSA—Oversight of vulnerable health center grantees (new)

We will determine the extent to which HRSA awards grant money to Health Center Program (HCP) grantees that have documented compliance or performance issues. HRSA has a variety of processes in place to monitor HCP grantees on program compliance, clinical performance, and financial health. However, even with all of these data available, HRSA may still continue to fund grantees with serious, ongoing compliance or performance issues. (OEI; 05-14-00470; expected issue date: FY 2015)

Indian Health Service

➤ IHS—Hospital oversight

We will examine IHS's efforts to ensure that its hospitals provide quality inpatient care. We will examine IHS's efforts to monitor each hospital's ability to provide quality care and maintain compliance with Medicare conditions of participation (CoP) and will identify which quality or compliance problems are most common. IHS operates 28 acute care hospitals that provide inpatient care to eligible American Indians and Alaska Natives. IHS hospitals are monitored through periodic onsite surveys by CMS-approved accrediting organizations that assess compliance with Medicare CoPs. (OEI; 09-13-00280; 06-14-00010; expected issue date: FY 2015)

National Institutes of Health

➤ NIH—Superfund financial activities for fiscal year 2014

We will review payments, obligations, reimbursements, and other uses of Superfund money by NIH's National Institute of Environmental Health Sciences. Federal law and regulations require that OIG conduct an annual audit of the Institute's Superfund activities. (Comprehensive Environmental Response, Compensation, and Liability Act of 1980, 42 U.S.C. § 9611(k).) (OAS; W-00-15-59050; expected issue date: FY 2015)

➤ NIH—Extramural construction grants

We will perform reviews at facilities that received extramural construction grants to determine whether funds were spent in accordance with Federal requirements. We will determine whether appropriate bidding procedures were followed and whether expenditures were allowable under the terms of the grants and applicable Federal requirements. Extramural construction grants are awarded to build, renovate, or repair non-Federal biomedical and behavioral research facilities. The intended recipients of these awards are institutions of higher education as well as nonprofit and regional organizations across the country. (42 CFR Part 52b, 45 CFR Part 74, 2 CFR Part 215, 2 CFR Part 220, and 2 CFR Part 225.) (OAS; W-00-13-50042; various reviews; expected issue date: FY 2015)

➤ NIH—Colleges' and universities' compliance with cost principles

We will assess colleges' and universities' compliance with selected cost principles issued by OMB in Circular A-21, *Cost Principles for Educational Institutions*. We will conduct reviews at selected colleges and universities on the basis of the dollar value of Federal grants received and on input from HHS operating divisions and the offices of the Assistant Secretary for Financial Resources and the Assistant Secretary for Administration. (OAS; W-00-13-50037; various reviews; expected issue date: FY 2015)

➤ NIH—Oversight of grants management policy implementation

We will examine NIH's oversight of three basic requirements for postaward grants administration among the 24 institutes and centers (ICs) that award extramural grants. We will also examine NIH's oversight of each IC's compliance with regulations, HHS directives, and agency policies. NIH issues grants administration policy to the ICs and oversees ICs' compliance with Federal regulations and HHS guidance. Each IC maintains a Grants Administration Office that implements its own procedures. Federal regulations establish uniform administrative requirements governing HHS grants. (45 CFR Parts 74 and 92.) The HHS *Grants Policy Directives* and the NIH *Grants Policy Statement* provide guidance on implementing the regulations. (OEI; 07-11-00190; expected issue date: FY 2015)

➤ NIH—Use of appropriated funds for contracting

We will review the appropriateness of NIH's obligation of appropriated funds for the services it obtains through contracts to ensure that appropriated funds were used only during their period of availability in accordance with the Anti-Deficiency Act of 1950 (Anti-Deficiency Act) and were used only for a bona fide need arising in the fiscal year for which the appropriation was made. We will review contracts and contract modifications to quantify any errors. Prior reviews identified problems in the use of appropriated funds for various NIH contracts. Key provisions of the Anti-Deficiency Act prohibit the Government from obligating or expending funds in advance of an appropriation unless authorized by law. (31 U.S.C § 1341(a)(1).) Also, appropriations may be used only for bona fide needs arising in the fiscal year for which the appropriation was made. (31 U.S.C. § 1502.) We will issue a summary report of corrective actions taken to address weaknesses identified in our reports. (OAS; W-00-10-52314; various reviews; expected issue date: FY 2015)

Substance Abuse and Mental Health Services Administration

➤ SAMHSA—Reporting and oversight of the Substance Abuse Prevention and Treatment Block Grant program performance

We will assess the data collection methods used by States to report on national outcome measures (NOMs) for the Substance Abuse Prevention and Treatment Block Grant (SAPTBG) program. We will also determine the extent to which SAMHSA oversees States' reporting of NOMs. SAMHSA is required to collect performance data and analyze the effectiveness of its programs, including the SAPTBG program. To do so, SAMHSA developed NOMs that aim to measure performance and improve accountability. However, SAMHSA has acknowledged a lack of specificity, uniformity, and quality in its data collection and reporting procedures. (OEI; 04-12-00160; expected issue date: FY 2015)

Other Public-Health-Related Reviews

➤ Audits of Hurricane Sandy Disaster Relief Act (new)

The Disaster Relief Appropriations Act, 2013, P.L. No. 113-2 (Disaster Relief Act), provided funding to HHS for use in aiding Hurricane Sandy disaster victims and their communities. After sequestration, HHS received $759.5 million in Disaster Relief Act funding. Of this amount, $733.6 million was allocated to three operating divisions: the Administration for Children and Families, NIH, and

SAMHSA. We plan to perform audits of grantees that have received Disaster Relief Act grant funding through one of the above-mentioned HHS operating divisions. We will review grantees' internal controls related to the oversight of Disaster Relief Act funds. Additionally, we plan to review the allowability of costs claimed and the appropriateness of costs that were budgeted but not yet expended. (OAS; W-00-15-59052; various reviews; expected issue date: FY 2015)

➤ Hurricane Sandy—HHS use of volunteer medical personnel to respond

We will describe the use of Medical Reserve Corps (MRC) volunteers in New Jersey and New York during the Hurricane Sandy response. We will also describe any challenges and successes encountered while using MRC volunteers. MRC is a national network of volunteers that is organized and managed at the local level. These volunteers provide various services, such as supporting local public health activities and assisting in emergency preparedness response and recovery. More than 2,000 volunteers were deployed in New York and New Jersey during the Hurricane Sandy response. (OEI; 04-13-00350; expected issue date: FY 2015)

➤ Hurricane Sandy—Social Services Block Grant guidance, disbursement, and reporting summary

We will assess guidance, disbursement, and reporting related to the $500 million in Hurricane Sandy disaster funding transferred to the Social Services Block Grant (SSBG). We will determine when HHS and States provided guidance to grantees regarding the expenditure of the funds, determine the timeliness with which HHS and States disbursed awards, and identify what reporting requirements were put in place. We will also describe challenges that States and their subgrantees encountered in accessing and using disaster funding. The Disaster Relief Act provided additional funds to the SSBG program to address necessary expenses resulting from Hurricane Sandy, including social, health, and mental health services for individuals and for repair, renovation, and rebuilding of health care facilities, child care facilities, and other social services facilities. (OEI; 00-00-00000; expected issue date: FY 2015)

➤ Hospitals' electronic health record system contingency plans (new)

We will determine the extent to which hospitals comply with contingency planning requirements of the Health Insurance Portability and Accountability Act (HIPAA). We will also compare hospitals' contingency plans with government- and industry-recommended practices. The HIPAA Security Rule requires covered entities to have a contingency plan that establishes policies and procedures for responding to an emergency or other occurrence that damages systems that contain protected health information (45 CFR, Part 164 § 308(7)(i)). (OEI; 01-14-00570; expected issue date: FY 2015)

Public Health Legal Activities

OIG assists the Department of Justice (DOJ) in resolving civil and administrative fraud cases and promoting compliance of HHS grantees. We assist DOJ in developing and pursuing Federal False Claims Act cases against institutions that receive grants from NIH and other public health service agencies. We also assist DOJ prosecutors in litigation and in settlement negotiations.

Violations of select agent requirements

In 2005, HHS issued a final regulation on possession, use, and transfer of select (biological) agents and toxins that applies to academic institutions; commercial manufacturing facilities; and Federal, State, and local laboratories. (70 Fed. Reg. 13294 (March 18, 2005), 42 CFR Part 73.) The rule authorizes OIG to conduct investigations and to impose civil monetary penalties against individuals or entities for violations of these requirements. We are continuing to coordinate efforts with CDC, the Federal Bureau of Investigation, and the Department of Agriculture to investigate violations of Federal requirements for the registration, storage, and transfer of select agents and toxins.

Human Services Reviews

The principal Department of Health and Human Services (HHS) agencies that administer human services programs are the:

- **Administration for Children and Families (ACF).** ACF operates over 30 programs that promote the economic and social well-being of children, families, and communities, including the Temporary Assistance for Needy Families (TANF) program; the national child support enforcement system; the Head Start program for preschool children; and assistance for child care, foster care, and adoption services.

- **Administration for Community Living (ACL).** ACL includes the Administration on Aging (AoA), which provides services such as meals, transportation, and caregiver support to older Americans at home and in the community through the nationwide network of services for the aging.

Effective management of these programs is essential to ensure that they achieve their goals and best serve the programs' intended beneficiaries. OIG's planning efforts for 2015 and beyond will focus on planning for emergencies, access to quality services, and compliance with safety requirements.

Acronyms and Abbreviations for Selected Terms:

ACF—Administration for Children and Families
ACL—Administration for Community Living
AoA—Administration on Aging
CSBG—Community Services Block Grant [program]

OCC—Office of Child Care
SMP—Senior Medicare Patrol
TANF—Temporary Assistance for Needy Families [program]

Descriptions of the Office of Inspector General's (OIG) human services work in progress for fiscal year (FY) 2015 follow.

Administration for Children and Families

➤ TANF—Compliance and oversight of work participation verification and reporting requirements

We will review the extent to which States comply with TANF work verification plan requirements. We will review ACF's oversight of States' compliance with work verification plan and reporting requirements. We will also assess ACF's oversight of tribes' compliance with Tribal Family Assistance Plan requirements under TANF. TANF provides assistance and work opportunities for needy families by granting States Federal funds and wide flexibility to develop and implement their own welfare programs. Regulations implementing the TANF program include, among other things, the requirement that States ensure that 50 percent of all funded families and 90 percent of two-parent families are working and that States report and verify work activities. (45 CFR Parts 261-265.) (OEI; 09-11-00490; 09-11-00491; expected issue date: FY 2015)

Foster care and adoption assistance maintenance payments

We will determine whether State agencies claimed foster care maintenance payments and adoption assistance payments in accordance with Federal requirements. Prior OIG audits found that States claimed costs for services that did not meet the requirements for the foster care and the adoption assistance programs. (Social Security Act, Title IV-E.) (OAS; W-00-13-24100; W-00-15-24100; various reviews; expected issue date: FY 2015)

Foster care—State oversight and coordination of health services for children

We will determine the extent to which States provide oversight and coordination of health services for children in foster care, as required. For selected States, we will determine the extent to which children in foster care receive health care services as outlined in States' health oversight and coordination plans. Each State is required to develop a plan for ongoing oversight and coordination of health care services for children in foster care (Fostering Connections to Success and Increasing Adoptions Act of 2008). States' plans must include certain elements, such as a schedule for initial and followup health screening and oversight of prescription medicines. (OEI; 07-13-00460; expected issue date: FY 2015)

Child support enforcement—Investigations under the child support enforcement task force model

We will continue to encourage and coordinate enforcement efforts in States, particularly in States that have not pursued prosecutions of nonsupport cases. Project Save Our Children seeks to identify, investigate, and prosecute individuals who fail to meet their court-ordered support obligations. The project brings together OIG, the U.S. Marshals Service, the Departments of Justice and State, local law enforcement agencies and prosecutors, State child support agencies, and others to enforce Federal and State criminal child support statutes.

Hurricane Sandy—Emergency preparedness and response plans for child care facilities (new)

We will determine the extent to which States develop and/or update emergency preparedness and response plans specific to child care services and programs. We will also describe emergency responses and experiences of States and child care providers during and after recent disasters. In February 2011, the Office of Child Care (OCC) in ACF recommended that States develop plans to address preparedness, response, and recovery efforts specific to child care services and programs. OCC outlined a framework that States should consider when developing and updating these plans. (OEI; 04-14-00410; expected issue date: FY 2016)

Head Start—Implementation of Head Start grant competition (new)

We will determine the extent to which Head Start grant competition resulted in new entities' competing for and winning Head Start grants in 2013 and 2014. The Improving Head Start for School Readiness Act of 2007 required that grantees be awarded 5-year (rather than indefinite) grants. Grantees who provide high-quality services receive future 5-year grants on a noncompetitive basis. Regulations at 45 CFR § 1307.3 describe seven deficiency conditions under the Designation Renewal System; if a grantee meets any of the seven conditions, it is not deemed a high-quality grantee and must compete for renewal. We will also describe the characteristics of grantees that were not deemed "high quality" by the Head Start Designation Renewal System in 2013 and 2014. (OEI; 12-14-00650; expected issue date: FY 2016)

Administration for Community Living

➢ ACL—Senior Medicare Patrol projects' performance data

We will review performance measures for Senior Medicare Patrol (SMP) projects, including documentation supporting expected recoveries for the Medicare and Medicaid programs. In 1997, SMP projects were established to recruit and train retired professionals and other senior citizens to recognize and report instances or patterns of health care fraud. The initiative stemmed from recommendations in a congressional committee report accompanying the Omnibus Consolidated Appropriations Act of 1997. OIG reports these performance data annually. The information was requested by AoA, which is part of ACL, and will support ACL's efforts to evaluate and improve the performance of the projects. (OEI; 00-00-00000; expected issue date: FY 2015)

Other HHS-Related Reviews

Certain financial, performance, and investigative issues cut across Department of Health and Human Services (HHS) programs. The Office of Inspector General's (OIG) work in progress and its planned work address Departmentwide matters, such as financial statement audits; financial accounting; information systems management; and other departmental issues, including discounted airfares and protections for people in residential settings who have disabilities.

Although we have discretion in allocating most of our non-Medicare and non-Medicaid resources, a portion is used for mandatory reviews, including financial statement audits conducted pursuant to the Government Management Reform Act of 1994 (GMRA), § 405(b); the Chief Financial Officers Act of 1990 (CFO Act); and information systems reviews required by the Federal Information Security Management Act of 2002 (FISMA).

The GMRA seeks to ensure that Federal managers have the financial information and flexibility necessary to make sound policy decisions and manage scarce resources. The GMRA broadened the CFO Act by requiring annual audited financial statements for all accounts and associated activities of HHS and other Federal agencies and components of Federal agencies, including the Centers for Medicare & Medicaid Services (CMS).

The American health care system is increasingly relying on health information technology (health IT) and the electronic exchange and use of health information. Health IT, including electronic health records, offers opportunities for improved patient care, more efficient practice management, and improved overall public health. OIG's future planning efforts may consider the significant challenges that exist with respect to overseeing expenditures for health IT, the interoperability and effective sharing and use of health care data for medical care, and emergency preparedness and response. Future work may also examine practices intended to protect sensitive information and the broad use of data and technology to manage HHS programs.

Acronyms and Abbreviations for Selected Terms:

AFR—Agency Financial Report
CFO Act—Chief Financial Officers Act of 1990
CMS—Centers for Medicare & Medicaid Services
FISMA—Federal Information Security Management Act of 2002
GAO—Government Accountability Office

GMRA—Government Management Reform Act of 1994
health IT—health information technology
IPERA— Improper Payment Elimination and Recovery Act of 2010
OMB—Office of Management and Budget

Financial Statement Audits and Related Reviews

> ## Audits of fiscal years 2014 and 2015 consolidated HHS financial statements and financial-related reviews

We will review the independent auditor's workpapers to determine whether financial statement audits of HHS and its components were conducted in accordance with Federal requirements. The purpose of a financial statement audit is to determine whether the financial statements present fairly, in all material respects, the financial position of the audited entity for the specified time period. (CFO, as amended by GMRA; Government Auditing Standards; and Office of Management and Budget (OMB) Bulletin 14-02, "Audit Requirements for Federal Financial Statements.") The audited consolidated fiscal years (FYs) 2014 and 2015 financial statements for HHS are due to OMB by November 17, 2014, and November 16, 2015, respectively. The audit reports on the HHS Special Purpose Financial Statements entered into the Governmentwide Financial Report System are intended to support the preparation of Governmentwide financial statements and reports. The report is prepared by the independent auditor, who audits the HHS Consolidated Financial Statements. We plan to perform a number of ancillary financial-related reviews related to the audits of the FYs 2014 and 2015 financial statements. The purpose of the financial-related reviews is to fulfill requirements in OMB Bulletin 14-02, "Audit Requirements for Federal Financial Statements," §§ 6.1 through 13. (OAS; W-00-14-40009; W-00-15-40009; A-17-14-00001; A-17-14-00006; A-17-15-00001; A-17-15-00006; expected issue dates: FY 2015 and FY 2016)

> ## Fiscal years 2014 and 2015 Centers for Medicare & Medicaid Services' financial statements

We will review the independent auditor's workpapers to determine whether the financial statement audit of the Centers for Medicare & Medicaid Services (CMS) was conducted in accordance with Federal requirements. The purpose of a financial statement audit is to determine whether the financial statements present fairly, in all material respects, the financial position of the audited entity for the specified time period. (CFO Act, as amended by the GMRA; Government Auditing Standards; and OMB Bulletin 14-02, "Audit Requirements for Federal Financial Statements.") (OAS; W-00-14-40008; W-00-15-40008; A-17-14-02014; A-17-15-02015; expected issue dates: FY 2015 and FY 2016)

Financial Reviews

> ## Compliance with reporting requirements for improper payments

We will review certain aspects of HHS's compliance with the Improper Payments Information Act of 2002, as amended, regarding reporting improper payments. We will also assess HHS's compliance with the Improper Payment Elimination and Recovery Act of 2010 (IPERA) and the data presented in HHS's Agency Financial Report (AFR) and provide recommendations for modifying the reporting and addressing the goals of the reporting requirements, as needed. Pursuant to the OMB Circular accompanying IPERA, OIG is required to review how HHS is assessing the programs it reports as well as the accuracy and completeness of the reporting in the AFR. IPERA requires the head of a Federal agency with programs or activities that may be susceptible to significant improper payments to report to Congress the agency's estimate of improper payments. For any program or activity with estimated improper payments exceeding $10 million and 1.5 percent, or $100 million regardless of the improper payment rate, the agency must report to Congress the actions that the agency is taking to reduce those payments. (OAS; W-00-12-40047; expected issue date: FY 2015)

Evaluation of predictive analytics for reducing improper payments

We will evaluate HHS's implementation of predictive analytics technologies and will assess HHS's reporting of actual and projected savings for improper payments avoided and recovered and the relative return on investment, and we will follow up on corrective actions made in response to our prior year's recommendations. We will also assess HHS's use of the technologies and determine whether improvements could be made to increase Medicare savings. The Small Business Jobs Act of 2010 required HHS to implement predictive analytics technologies for reducing improper payments in Medicare fee for service. HHS must report annually on the progress of the programs and certify certain amounts it reports. (OAS; W-00-14-40060; W-00-15-40060; various reviews; expected issue date: FY 2015)

HHS contract management review

We will review the controls the HHS Program Support Center has in place to ensure compliance with requirements specified in appropriations statutes when awarding contracts. We will review HHS's quality assurance procedures to determine the accuracy and completeness of the internal control reviews to ensure full compliance with appropriations laws. HHS, in its July 2011 *Antideficiency Report to the President,* noted that it implemented corrective actions, including adopting quality assurance procedures and conducting procurement management and internal control reviews to validate full compliance with appropriations laws and regulations to ensure that there would be no future violations of the Anti-Deficiency Act. (31 U.S.C. § 1341(a)(1) and Bona Fide Needs Rule.) (31 U.S.C. § 1502).) (OAS; W-00-13-52313; expected issue date: FY 2015)

HHS agencies' annual accounting of drug-control funds

We will review HHS agencies' compliance with the requirement that agencies expending funds on National Drug Control Program activities submit to the Office of National Drug Control Policy an annual accounting of the expenditure of such funds. (21 U.S.C. § 1704.) The policy also requires that an agency submit with its annual accounting an authentication by the agency's OIG in which OIG expresses a conclusion on the reliability of the agency's assertions in its accounting. We will submit this authentication with respect to HHS's FY 2014 annual accounting. (OAS; W-00-15-41020; various reviews; expected issue date: FY 2015)

OIG reviews of non-Federal audits

We will continue to review the quality of audits conducted by non-Federal auditors, such as public accounting firms and State auditors, in accordance with OMB Circular A-133, *Audits of States, Local Governments, and Non-Profit Organizations.* State, local, and Indian tribal governments; colleges and universities; and nonprofit organizations receiving Federal awards are required to have annual organizationwide audits of all Federal funds that they receive. Our reviews ensure that the audits and reports meet applicable standards, identify any followup work needed, and identify issues that may require management attention. OIG also provides upfront technical assistance to non-Federal auditors to ensure that they understand Federal audit requirements and to promote effective audit work. We analyze and record electronically the audit findings reported by non-Federal auditors for use by HHS managers. Our reviews inform HHS managers about the management of Federal programs and identify significant areas of internal control weaknesses, noncompliance with laws and regulations, and questioned costs that require formal resolution by Federal officials. (OAS; W-00-00-0000; various reviews; expected issue date: FY 2015)

➤ OIG reimbursable audits of non-HHS funds

We will conduct a series of audits as part of HHS's cognizant-agency responsibility under OMB Circular A-133, *Audits of States, Local Governments, and Non-Profit Organizations*. HHS OIG has audit cognizance over all State governments and most major research colleges and universities that receive Federal funds. We enter into agreements with other Federal audit organizations or other Federal agencies to reimburse us as the cognizant audit organization for audits that we perform of non-HHS funds. To ensure a coordinated Federal approach to audits of colleges, universities, and States, OMB establishes audit cognizance, that is, it designates which Federal agency has primary responsibility for audit of all Federal funds the entity receives. (OAS; W-00-15-50012; various reviews; expected issue date: FY 2015)

➤ Requests for audit services

Throughout the year, Congress, HHS, and other Federal organizations request that we perform a variety of financial-related audit services, including contract and grant closeouts, indirect cost audits, bid proposal audits, and other reviews designed to provide specific information requested by management. We evaluate requests as we receive them, considering such factors as why the audit is being requested, how the results will be used, when the results are needed, and whether the work is cost beneficial. (OAS; W-00-15-41021; various reviews; expected issue date: FY 2015)

Automated Information Systems

➤ HHS compliance with the Federal Information Security Management Act of 2002

We will review various HHS operating divisions' compliance with FISMA. FISMA and OMB Circular A-130, *Management of Federal Information Resources*, Appendix III, require that agencies and their contractors maintain programs that provide adequate security for all information collected, processed, transmitted, stored, or disseminated in general support systems and major applications. (OAS; W-00-14-40016; W-00-15-40016; W-00-14-42001; W-00-15-42001; various reviews; expected issue date: FY 2015)

➤ Penetration testing of HHS and operating division networks

We will conduct network and Web application penetration testing to determine HHS's and its operating divisions' network security posture and determine whether these networks and applications are susceptible to hackers. Penetration tests are used to identify methods of gaining access to a system by using tools and techniques known to be employed by hackers. There has been an increase in activity from computer hacker groups compromising government systems and releasing sensitive data to the public or using such data to commit fraud. (OAS; W-00-14-42020; W-00-15-42020; various reviews; expected issue date: FY 2015)

Other HHS-Related Issues

➢ HHS efforts to address grantee risks

We will determine how HHS awarding agencies mitigate grantee risks and whether HHS awarding agencies receive and/or share information on grantees for which they have concerns regarding performance expectations and/or accountability requirements. HHS is the largest grant-making agency in the Federal Government. In FY 2013, HHS awarded nearly $344 billion in grants. Oversight of these funds is crucial to HHS's mission and to the health and well-being of the public. Federal regulations incorporate uniform administrative requirements governing HHS awards. Guidance in implementing those regulatory requirements is contained in the HHS *Grants Policy Directives*, which apply across HHS. (OEI; 07-12-00110; expected issue date: FY 2015)

➢ Prevent grant awards to individuals and entities who were suspended and/or debarred (new)

We will determine whether HHS operating divisions are taking adequate precautions to ensure that individuals and entities suspended or debarred are not awarded Federal grants or contracts. To protect the Government's interests, Federal agencies are required to make awards only to responsible sources—those that are determined to be reliable, dependable, and capable of performing required work. One way to protect the Government's interests is through suspensions and debarments, which are actions taken to preclude firms or individuals from receiving contracts or assistance because of various types of misconduct. A suspension is a temporary exclusion typically pending the completion of an investigation or legal proceeding, while a debarment is for a fixed term that depends on the seriousness of the cause, but generally is for a period of 3 years. These exclusions are reported in the System for Award Management (SAM), maintained by the General Services Administration, along with violations of certain statutes and regulations. A previous report by the Government Accountability Office (GAO) found that some agency programs need greater attention, and governmentwide oversight could be improved. (OAS; W-00-15-59024; expected issue date: FY 2015)

➢ HHS's Government purchase, travel, and integrated charge card programs

We will review HHS's charge card programs (e.g., purchase, travel, or integrated cards) to assess the risks of illegal, improper, or erroneous purchases. OMB has instructed IGs to submit annual status reports on purchase and travel card audit recommendations beginning January 31, 2014, for compilation and transmission to Congress and GAO. Further, IGs are required to conduct periodic risk assessments of their agencies' charge card programs to analyze the risks of illegal, improper, or erroneous purchases. (Government Charge Card Abuse Prevention Act of 2012 (Charge Card Act).) The Charge Card Act requires IGs to use the risk assessments to determine the necessary scope, frequency, and number of IG audits or reviews of the charge card programs. It requires Federal agencies, including HHS, to establish and maintain safeguards and internal controls for purchase cards (including convenience checks), travel cards, and integrated cards. HHS's charge card programs enable cardholders to pay for commercial goods, services, and travel expenses. This risk assessment will determine the extent and focus of our subsequent audit efforts. (OAS; W-00-15-00000; expected issue date: FY 2015)

Appendixes

Affordable Care Act Reviews

The Office of Inspector General (OIG) is focused on promoting the economy, efficiency, and effectiveness of Affordable Care Act[1] programs across the Department of Health and Human Services (HHS or the Department). The ACA vested in the Department substantial responsibilities for increasing access to health insurance for those who are eligible for coverage, improving access to and the quality of health care, and lowering health care costs and increasing value for taxpayers and patients. OIG's ongoing and planned reviews for fiscal year (FY) 2015 will assess the Department's implementation and operation of ACA programs and progress toward achieving program goals. To this end, we are prioritizing work in three main areas: the health insurance marketplaces, including financial assistance payments; Medicare and Medicaid reforms; and grant expenditures for public health programs.

In addition to performing the specific work described below, OIG is committed in FY 2015 to initiating at least 5-10 additional reviews addressing ACA programs. These reviews could focus on emerging marketplace issues, including, for example, potential vulnerabilities that may arise in connection with the second open enrollment period; implementation of additional marketplace functionality, such as the redetermination process; or the premium stabilization programs. They could also focus on other ACA areas, including Medicaid expansion, new Medicare payment and delivery models, or new grant programs. OIG experts dedicated to ACA work planning will employ a dynamic and flexible planning process that incorporates continuous risk assessment and stakeholder input, among other factors, to identify the most critical areas for additional reviews and the most appropriate methodologies to deliver timely and relevant results. As appropriate, we will work with other Federal and State oversight agencies to address emerging vulnerabilities. For example, we are working jointly with the Treasury Inspector General for Tax Administration (TIGTA) on work examining controls and processes for the Advance Premium Tax Credit and Premium Tax Credit programs.

Acronyms and Abbreviations for Selected Terms:

APTC— Advanced Premium Tax Credit
CMS—Centers for Medicare & Medicaid Services
CO-OP—Consumer Operated and Oriented Plan
CSR—Cost Sharing Reduction

FFM—Federally Facilitated Marketplace
HRSA—Health Services and Resources Administration
TIGTA—Treasury Inspector General for Tax Administration

Health Insurance Marketplaces, Financial Assistance Payments, and Market Stabilization Payments

OIG's FY 2015 oversight strategy for the marketplaces and related programs continues our focus on proper expenditure of taxpayer funds and the efficient and effective operation of the marketplaces. To

---

[1] The Patient Protection and Affordable Care Act of 2010 (ACA), as amended by the Health Care and Education Reconciliation Act of 2010 (P.L. 111-148).

this end, in FY 2015 we will continue to address key risks in the areas of payments, eligibility and enrollment, management and administration of marketplace programs, and security of information technology and consumer information. Many reviews will address questions in multiple areas.

Payments—Are taxpayer funds being expended correctly for their intended purposes?

Ongoing and planned FY 2015 work looking at expenditures of taxpayer funds includes:

> **Accuracy of aggregate payments to qualified health plan issuers for advanced premium tax credits and cost sharing reductions and effectiveness of related internal controls**

ACA, §§ 1401, 1402, 1411, 1412. We will determine the accuracy of aggregate financial assistance payments – Advanced Premium Tax Credit (APTC) and Cost Sharing Reduction (CSR) – made to qualified health plan issuers, and assess the related internal controls governing how those financial assistance amounts are calculated in accordance with Federal requirements. Payment amounts vary according to income, marital status, household composition, and eligibility for Government-sponsored or employer-sponsored health care coverage. This work will focus on the systems managed by HHS to make these payments. Under the system, the Centers for Medicare & Medicaid Services (CMS) makes financial assistance payments to issuers on the basis of aggregate enrollee information for each qualified health plan. (OAS; W-00-14-59018; various reviews; expected issue date: FY 2015)

> **Accuracy of Advance Premium Tax Credits and Cost Sharing Reductions payments for individual enrollees (new)**

ACA, §§ 1401, 1402, 1411, 1412. We will determine the accuracy of financial assistance payments—APTC and CSR—for individual enrollees. Specifically, we will (1) verify financial assistance payment amounts calculated by the marketplaces, (2) confirm the payment of monthly premiums for individuals to remain eligible to receive financial assistance payments, (3) determine any subsequent changes in eligibility status affecting calculated financial assistance payment amounts, and (4) reconcile estimated financial assistance payments made to actual payment amounts. Payment amounts vary according to income, marital status, household composition, and eligibility for Government-sponsored or employer-sponsored health care coverage. This work will focus on the processes and controls in place to make and ensure the accuracy of financial assistance payments for individual enrollees. (OAS; W-00-15-59048; various reviews; expected issue date: FY 2015)

> **CMS's internal controls over Advance Premium Tax Credit obligations and payments Under the Affordable Care Act (new)**

ACA, §§ 1401, 1402, 1411, and 1412. We will determine whether CMS has established adequate accountability and internal controls for generating, reviewing, and approving advance premium tax credit payments. We will assess CMS's process for obtaining premium tax credit information from issuers and subsequent processes for providing payment data to the Department of the Treasury. We will also assess the coordination processes between CMS and the Internal Revenue Service (IRS) to ensure that Advance Premium Tax Credits are accurate and are made to eligible policyholders. This review is part of a joint project with TIGTA. (OAS; W-00-15-59045; various reviews; expected issue date: FY 2015)

> **Programmatic justification for CMS's involvement in Premium Tax Credit obligations under the Affordable Care Act (new)**

ACA, §§ 1401, 1402, 1411, and 1412. We will describe CMS's involvement in Premium Tax Credit obligations and programmatic justification for structuring program responsibilities in such a manner between CMS and IRS. (OEI; 06-14-00590; expected issue date: FY 2015)

> **Review of Affordable Care Act establishment grants for State marketplaces (new)**

ACA, § 1311. We will determine whether nine States complied with Federal requirements related to the development and implementation of a State marketplace in accordance with the terms and conditions of Federal cooperative agreements. The ACA authorized funding to States that elected to establish their own marketplaces. Several of these States encountered significant problems in the launching of their marketplaces. As part of the review, we will assess whether Federal funds were used as intended and whether the State agencies' procurement process and internal controls for monitoring and oversight were effective. We will also review policies and procedures issued by CMS to State agencies relating to establishment grants for marketplaces. (OAS; W-00-14-59034; various reviews; expected issue date: FY 2015)

> **Payments to Federally Facilitated Marketplace contractors**

This review will examine HHS payments to contractors for work on the Federally Facilitated Marketplace (FFM). We plan to address key questions, including whether performance-based contracting was used to determine payments to contractors, whether contractors received incentive payments, whether contractor invoices met requirements, and whether contractors were paid appropriately. (OAS; W-00-14-59030; A-03-14-03001; expected issue date: FY 2015).

> **Consumer Operated and Oriented Plan Loan Program—Eligibility status and use of startup and solvency loans**

ACA, § 1322. We will follow up on prior OIG work that examined the selection process for Consumer Operated and Oriented Plan (CO-OP) loans and identified factors that could affect the CO-OP loan program, including startup funding levels. In this new work, we will conduct a series of audits to verify CO-OP eligibility status and the use of startup and solvency loans. (OAS; W-00-14-59019; various reviews, expected issue date: FY 2015)

> **Review of Grant Awards to Navigators in Federally Facilitated or State Partnership Marketplaces (new)**

ACA, § 1311. We will determine whether navigators in FFM or State partnership marketplaces met the required qualifications and costs allowable under the terms of the grants and applicable Federal regulations. Under the ACA, marketplaces are to establish a program under which it awards grants to entities that facilitate education about and enrollment in qualified health plans. These organizations are known as navigators. As part of our review, we will determine whether navigators completed the required training, criminal background checks, and State training and registration before assisting consumers. We will also review costs claimed to determine whether they were allowable and were claimed in accordance with the terms of the grant awards and Federal regulations. (OAS; W-00-15-59047; various reviews; expected issue date: FY 2015)

Eligibility—Are the right people getting the right benefits?

OIG's FY 2015 work reviewing the effectiveness and efficiency of marketplace eligibility and enrollment systems includes:

> ### ➢ Review of Affordable Care Act enrollment safeguards at additional State marketplaces (new)

ACA, § 1411. In FY 2014, OIG issued two reports that identified vulnerabilities in eligibility and enrollment systems at the FFM and State-based marketplaces. Our new work will assess the effectiveness of internal controls in place at seven State-based marketplaces to ensure that accurate information is used to determine consumer eligibility for enrollment and financial assistance payments. We will determine whether internal controls implemented by the selected marketplaces were effective in ensuring that individuals were enrolled in a qualified health plan (QHP) according to Federal requirements. Using a statistically valid sample of applicants, we will review whether each marketplace has performed the required verifications to determine eligibility for enrollment in a QHP and has appropriately resolved inconsistencies between applicant information and data sources used for verification. (OAS; W-00-14-42024; various reviews; expected issue date: FY 2015)

> ### ➢ Review of the Federally Facilitated Marketplace's eligibility verifications for Premium Tax Credits (new)

ACA, §§ 1411 and 1412. We will assess whether the FFM's internal controls were effective in ensuring that individuals were eligible for the Premium Tax Credit in accordance with Federal regulations. The FFM is required to verify an applicant's information, including household income, to determine his or her eligibility for Premium Tax Credit. Using a statistically valid sample of applicants, we will review whether the FFM performed the required verifications when determining applicants' eligibility for Premium Tax Credits and resolved inconsistencies between applicant information and data sources used for verification. We will examine the FFM's procedures for verifying an applicant's information, which includes household income, using data provided to the FFM by IRS and other sources. This work is planned to supplement a prior OIG review related to enrollment safeguards mandated by the Continuing Appropriations Act (CAA), 2014, § 1001(c). We are working, in consultation with IRS, to develop similar reviews at State marketplaces. (OAS; W-00-15-59046; various reviews; expected issue date: FY 2015)

> ### ➢ Inconsistencies in the Federally Facilitated Marketplace applicant data

We will determine the extent to which CMS was able to resolve inconsistencies between applicant self-attested information and data received through Federal and other data sources that occurred in the 2013-2014 open enrollment period of the FFM. We will also assess the extent to which CMS's new processes are resolving inconsistencies between applicant information and data sources used for verification. We will update this analysis of the FFM for the 2014-2015 open enrollment period. Previous OIG work found that the FFM was unable to resolve 2.6 million out of 2.9 million inconsistencies because CMS's eligibility system was not fully operational. (OEI; 01-14-00620, expected issue date: FY 2016)

Additional work examining Medicaid eligibility systems is described in the "Medicaid Reviews" section below.

Management and Administration—Is the Department managing and administering marketplace programs effectively and efficiently?

OIG's work in this area includes:

➤ Implementation of the Federally Facilitated Marketplace

We will review the Department's overall efforts in implementing the FFM. We will conduct document reviews and interviews to assess strengths and weaknesses found with CMS management and its use of contractors. The difficulties encountered during the launch of the FFM on October 1, 2013, raised serious concerns about the planning, management, and oversight of the FFM project. Our review will include an assessment of management and operational changes made after the launch and CMS implementation of the second open enrollment period, scheduled to begin November 15, 2014. (OEI; 06-14-00350; expected issue date: FY 2015)

➤ Acquisition planning and procurement for the Federally Facilitated Marketplace

We will determine whether HHS performed required acquisition planning and oversight activities for FFM contracts. We will also describe HHS's procurement process for selecting FFM contractors. Acquisition planning and procurement were among the critical steps to ensuring the FFM's success. (OEI; 03-14-00230; expected issue date: FY 2015)

➤ Oversight of Federally Facilitated Marketplace contractors

This review will examine whether HHS exercised appropriate and adequate oversight and direction over contracts related to the FFM (including mechanisms that HHS and its contractors used to communicate problems or concerns about the FFM); whether HHS complied with oversight and monitoring requirements required by Federal and HHS regulations; and whether contractors individually and as a whole met requirements of their contracts, the acquisition plan, and the ACA. (OAS; W-00-14-59032; A-03-14-03003; expected issue date: FY 2015)

Security—Is consumers' personal information safe?

Reviews underway to address security in the Marketplaces include:

➤ CMS's implementation of security controls over consumer information obtained in the Federally Facilitated Marketplace

We previously conducted a review of information system security of HealthCare.gov. In this review, we will determine whether information security controls for the systems outside the FFM containing and storing consumer information have been implemented in accordance with Federal requirements and recognized industry best practices. We may conduct vulnerability scans, when feasible, using automated tools that seek to identify known security vulnerabilities and discover possible methods of attack that can lead to unauthorized access or the exfiltration of data. We will also review any reports related to prior vulnerability assessments and determine whether the vulnerabilities identified were remediated in a timely manner. (OAS; W-00-14-42023; expected issue date: FY 2015)

> **State-based marketplaces information system security controls**

We previously conducted reviews of information system security at two State-based marketplaces. We will determine whether information security controls for additional State-based marketplaces have been implemented in accordance with Federal requirements and recognized industry best practices. We will conduct vulnerability scans of Web-based systems using automated tools that seek to identify known security vulnerabilities and discover possible methods of attack that can lead to unauthorized access or the exfiltration of data. We will also review any reports related to prior vulnerability assessments of State-based marketplace systems and determine whether the vulnerabilities identified were remediated in a timely manner. (OAS; W-00-14-42025; W-00-15-42025; various reviews; expected issue date: FY 2015)

Also, in coordination with other law enforcement partners, OIG is monitoring for reports of cybersecurity threats and consumer fraud. OIG has promoted, and will continue to promote, consumer awareness and prevention of fraud in the marketplaces, including, for example, identity theft, imposter marketers, and fake Web sites. Additional information about consumer protection can be found at: http://oig.hhs.gov/fraud/consumer-alerts/index.asp.

Medicaid and Medicare Reforms

Medicaid Reviews

The Medicaid section of the *Work Plan* describes the range of FY 2015 reviews planned and those in progress to promote the effectiveness and efficiency of the growing Medicaid program. Focus areas include prescription drugs; billing, payment, reimbursement, quality, and safety of home health services, community-based care, and other services, equipment, and supplies; State management of Medicaid, information system controls and security; and Medicaid managed care.

Reviews related directly to specific ACA provisions include the following (these reviews are described more fully in the Medicaid section of the *Work Plan*):

> **Enhanced Federal Medical Assistance Percentage**

ACA, § 2001. (OAS; W-00-14-31480; various reviews; expected issue date: FY 2015) *Work Plan* page 35.

> **Medicaid eligibility determinations in selected States**

ACA, § 2001. (OAS; W-00-14-31140; W-00-15-31140; OEI; 06-14-00330; various reviews; expected issue date: FY 2015) *Work Plan* page 36.

> **Community First Choice State plan option under the Affordable Care Act (new)**

ACA, § 2401. (OAS; W-00-15-00000; A-02-15-00000; expected issue date: FY 2016) *Work Plan* page 33.

> **States' experiences with enhanced provider screening**

ACA § 6402. (OEI; 05-13-00520; expected issue date: FY 2015) *Work Plan* page 38.

> **Provider payment suspensions during pending investigations of credible fraud allegations**

ACA, § 6402(h)(2). (OAS; W-00-14-31473; various reviews; expected issue date: FY 2015; OEI; 09-14-00020; expected issue date: FY 2015) *Work Plan* page 38.

> **State terminations of providers terminated by Medicare or by other States**

ACA, § 6501. (OEI; 06-12-00030; expected issue date: FY 2015) *Work Plan* page 37.

> **Completeness and accuracy of managed care encounter data**

ACA, § 6504. (OEI; 07-13-00120; expected issue date: FY 2015) *Work Plan* page 41.

> **National Correct Coding Initiative edits and CMS oversight**

ACA, § 6507. (OAS; W-00-15-31459; various reviews; expected issue date: FY 2015; OEI; 00-00-0000; expected issue date: FY 2015) *Work Plan* page 39.

> **Payments to States under the Balancing Incentive Program (new)**

ACA , § 10202. (OAS; W-00-15-31482; various reviews; expected issue date: FY 2016) *Work Plan* page 33.

> **State collection of rebates for drugs dispensed to Medicaid managed care organization enrollees (new)**

ACA, § 2501(c). (OAS; W-00-14-31483; W-00-15-31483; various reviews; expected issue date: FY 2015) *Work Plan* page 29.

> **States' collection and reporting of rebates**

ACA, § 2501. (OEI; 03-12-00520; expected issue date: FY 2015) *Work Plan* page 29.

> **Comparison of Medicare Part D and Medicaid pharmacy reimbursement and rebates**

ACA, § 2501. (OEI; 03-13-00650; expected issue date: FY 2015) *Work Plan* page 30.

> **Health-care-acquired conditions—Prohibition on Federal reimbursements**

ACA, § 2702. (OAS; W-00-14-31452; various reviews; expected issue date: FY 2015) *Work Plan* page 32.

Medicare Reviews

The ACA introduced changes to the Medicare program designed to improve efficiency and quality of care and promote program integrity and transparency. The Medicare sections of the FY 2015 *Work Plan* describe OIG's on-going and planned reviews of all parts of the Medicare program. Much of this work will provide data and information on cost, quality, and delivery of Medicare services that can aid the

Department as it develops new, value-driven payment and delivery models for the Medicare program, including those being implemented pursuant to the ACA.

The following reviews address specific ACA provisions related to the Medicare program and are described in more detail in the Medicare sections of the Work Plan:

> **Hospice in assisted living facilities**

ACA, § 3132. (OEI; 02-14-00070; expected issue date: FY 2015) *Work Plan* page 9.

> **Quality of sponsor data used in calculating coverage-gap discounts**

ACA, § 3301. (OAS; W-00-14-35611; various reviews; expected issue date: FY 2015) *Work Plan* page 27.

> **Ensuring dual eligibles' access to drugs under Part D**

ACA, § 3313. (OEI; 00-00-00000; expected issue date: FY 2015) *Work Plan* page 26.

> **Program for national background checks for long-term-care employees**

ACA, § 6201. (OEI; 07-10-00420; expected issue date: FY 2017) *Work Plan* page 8.

> **Enhanced enrollment screening process for Medicare providers**

ACA, § 6401. (OEI; 03-13-00050; expected issue date: FY 2015) *Work Plan* page 22.

> **Risk Assessment of CMS's Administration of the Pioneer Accountable Care Organization Model (new)**

ACA, § 3021. (OAS; W-00-00-00000; expected issue date: FY 2015) *Work Plan* page 23.

Other Programs

OIG work in this area includes:

> **Prevention and Public Health Fund grants—Centers for Disease Control and Prevention oversight**

ACA, § 4002. (OAS; W-00-14-59027; expected issue date: FY 2015) *Work Plan* page 49.

> **Health Services and Resources Administration (HRSA)—Community health centers' compliance with grant requirements of the Affordable Care Act (new)**

ACA, § 10503. (OAS; W-00-14-59028; W-00-15-59028; various reviews, expected issue dates: FY 2015) *Work Plan* page 51.

> **HRSA—Duplicate discounts for 340B-purchased drugs (new)**

ACA, § 2501. (OEI; 05-14-00430; expected issue date: FY 2015) *Work Plan* page 51.

Recovery Act Reviews

Pursuant to the American Recovery and Reinvestment Act of 2009 (Recovery Act), the Office of Inspector General (OIG) received funding for discretionary oversight of programs and operations of the Department of Health and Human Services (HHS) that received supplemental funding through the Recovery Act. The funds have been used primarily to conduct financial oversight activities to ensure that HHS agencies and grantees used the funds they received for the intended purposes and in accordance with established requirements. Recovery Act funding resulted in a significant increase in the number of grants and contracts awarded by HHS. The reviews that follow represent OIG's continuing oversight of HHS agencies' use of Recovery Act funds.

Acronyms and Abbreviations for Selected Terms:

CMS—Centers for Medicare & Medicaid Services   EHR—electronic health records

Medicare and Medicaid

Adoption of Electronic Health Records

An EHR is an electronic record of health-related information for an individual that is generated by health care providers. It may include a patient's health history, along with other items.

> **Medicare incentive payments for adopting electronic health records**
>
> We will review Medicare incentive payments to eligible health care professionals and hospitals for adopting EHRs and the Centers for Medicare & Medicaid Services (CMS) safeguards to prevent erroneous incentive payments. We will review Medicare incentive payment data from 2011 to identify payments to providers that should not have received incentive payments (e.g., those not meeting selected meaningful use criteria). We will also assess CMS's plans to oversee incentive payments for the duration of the program and corrective actions taken regarding erroneous incentive payments. Medicare incentive payments are authorized over a 5-year period to physicians and hospitals that demonstrate meaningful use of certified EHR technology. (Recovery Act, §§ 4101 and 4102.) Incentive payments were scheduled to begin in 2011 and continue through 2016, with payment reductions to health care professionals who fail to become meaningful users of EHRs beginning in 2015. (§ 4101(b).) As of August 2014, Medicare EHR incentive payments totaled more than $16 billion. (OAS; W-00-14-31352; expected issue date: FY 2015; Recovery Act)

> **Medicaid incentive payments for adopting electronic health records**

We will review Medicaid incentive payments to Medicaid providers and hospitals for adopting electronic health records (EHRs) and CMS safeguards to prevent erroneous incentive payments. We will determine whether incentive payments to Medicaid providers to purchase, implement, and operate EHR technology were claimed in accordance with Medicaid requirements; assess CMS's actions to remedy erroneous incentive payments and its plans for securing the payments for the duration of the incentive program; and determine whether payments to States for related administrative expenses were appropriate. The law authorizes 100 percent Federal financial participation for allowable expenses for eligible Medicaid providers to purchase, implement, and operate certified EHR technology. (Recovery Act § 4201.) The section also provides a 90-percent Federal match for State administrative expenses for the adoption of certified EHR technology by Medicaid providers. As of August 2014, Medicaid EHR incentive payments totaled more than $8 billion. Incentive payments will continue through 2021. (OAS; W-00-13-31351; W-00-14-31351; various reviews; expected issue date: FY 2015; Recovery Act)

Systems and Information Security

> **Security of certified electronic health record technology under meaningful use**

We will perform audits of various covered entities receiving EHR incentive payments from CMS and their business associates, such as EHR cloud service providers, to determine whether they adequately protect electronic health information created or maintained by certified EHR technology. A core meaningful-use objective for eligible providers and hospitals is to protect electronic health information created or maintained by certified EHR technology by implementing appropriate technical capabilities. To meet and measure this objective, eligible hospitals, including critical access hospitals, must conduct a security risk analysis of certified EHR technology as defined in Federal regulations and use the capabilities and standards of Certified Electronic Health Record Technology. (45 CFR § 164.308(a)(1) and 45 CFR §§ 170.314(d)(1) – (d)(9).) Furthermore, business associates that transmit, process, and store EHRs for Medicare and Medicaid providers are playing a larger role in the protection of electronic health information. Therefore, audits of cloud service providers and other downstream service providers are necessary to ensure compliance with regulatory requirements and contractual agreements. (OAS; W-00-14-42020; W-00-15-42020; various reviews; expected issue date: FY 2015; Recovery Act)

Cross-Cutting Enforcement Activities

OIG conducts criminal investigations of referrals of grant and contract fraud in the misuse of Recovery Act funds and with regard to reprisals against whistleblowers.

Fraud and Whistleblower Reprisals

> **Integrity of Recovery Act expenditures**

We will continue to evaluate credible allegations of improper expenditures of Recovery Act funds to identify cases in which criminal investigations should be opened and enforcement actions pursued. Recovery Act funding resulted in a significant increase in the number of grants and contracts awarded by HHS. The Recovery Act requires transparency and accountability in the awarding and spending of funds. (OI; various investigations; Recovery Act)

➤ **Enforcement of whistleblower protections**

We will continue to evaluate credible allegations of reprisals against whistleblowers by entities or individuals receiving Recovery Act funds to identify cases in which criminal investigations should be opened and antireprisal enforcement actions pursued. The Recovery Act extends whistleblower protection to employees who reasonably believe they are being retaliated against for reporting misuse of Recovery Act funds received by their non-Federal employers. (Recovery Act, § 1553.) (OI; various investigations; Recovery Act)